PORTFOLIO PEOPLE

For Jo

Portfolio People

How to Create a Workstyle as Individual as You Are

Max Comfort

CENTURY
BUSINESS

First published in the United Kingdom in 1997 by Century Ltd
Random House, 20 Vauxhall Bridge Road, London SW1V 2SA

Random House Australia (Pty) Limited
16 Dalmore Drive, Scoresby, Victoria 3179
Australia

Random House New Zealand Limited
18 Poland Road, Glenfield, Auckland 10
New Zealand

Random House South Africa (Pty) Limited
PO Box 2263, Rosebank 2121
South Africa

Random House UK Limited Reg No. 954009
Papers used by Random House UK are natural, recyclable products made from
wood grown in sustainable forests. The manufacturing processes conform to the
environmental regulations of the country of origin.

Companies, institutions and other organizations wishing to make bulk
purchases of any business books published by Random House should
contact their local bookstore or Random House direct:
Special Sales Director
Random House, 20 Vauxhall Bridge Road, London SW1V 2SA

Tel. 0171 973 9000   Fax 0171 828 6681

ISBN 0 7126 7727 5
Typeset by Deltatype Ltd, Birkenhead, Merseyside
Printed and bound in Great Britain by
Mackays of Chatham plc, Chatham, Kent

About the Author

Max Comfort trained as an architect at the Architectural Association at the time of Archigram's plug-in cities, student riots and flower power. He has designed mile-wide geodesic domes for Eskimos, mansions for Mick Jagger, flats for old age pensioners, recording studios for the music industry and exceedingly large office blocks for exceedingly large property developers. He also had a go at the National Gallery but Prince Charles put a stop to it.

In the early '80s, working out of a luxury motorhome, Max became a roving spiritual and intentional community planner in the Pacific Northwest, using meditation and intuition to plot drains, roads, homes and temples. Back in the UK, having experienced at first hand the excesses of the Thatcher years, he embarked on the task of integrating Spirit into Business, using his long experience of personal development to lead workshops and trainings, among them the Max Comfort Masterclass, an intuition led exploration of the relationship between self and work.

He is now one of the UK's first *holistic* business consultants, using strategies and methods based on his own philosophy for the ethical resolution of problems. He sees no difficulty in using spiritual principles on banks or the VAT man – but he may not always let them know! A qualified massage practitioner, he delivers the integration of personal development, alternative therapies and sound, traditional business advice. Work, for Max, isn't just about making money, it's very much about personal growth. Current trends in the workplace support this view.

A great supporter of the Dalai Lama, Max is chair and co-founder of ApTibet, a charity set up to provide simple and appropriate technologies for Tibetan refugees in India. He has two grown up children, one studying and one surfing in Kauai. He lives with his partner in Muswell Hill, London and enjoys fetching fresh croissants from the local patisserie on Sunday mornings.

He is the co-author of *The A to Zen of Life Maintenance*, a self-development book based on the effective use of intuition.

Contents

Acknowledgements

In an era strong on cleverness and light on wisdom, I'd like to acknowledge the wise people I've come across, either in person or in print. Foremost among these and central to this book is Professor Charles Handy, who I believe first coined the phrase 'Portfolio Career' and whose inspiring humanity and far-sightedness set the whole process of this book in motion.

A big 'thank you' is due to Francis Kinsman, for the tremendous range of his insights and also for his Foreword. To George Ripley, who has a pearl for every time we meet, Andrew Ferguson for his single-mindeness, John Naisbitt for his extraordinary breadth of vision, William Bridges for his thoroughness and clarity, Malidoma Somé for reminding me of my source, Peter Caddy for his courageous humility, His Holiness the 14th Dalai Lama for his contagious sense of humour, Michael Meade for his wonderful way of storytelling and Paulo Coelho for his ability to lovingly refine complexity into simplicity.

This book would not have been written without the enormous enthusiasm and encouragement of Gillian Edwards, for a time my co-presenter of workshops on Portfolio Working. Nor would it have come about without all the participants on *Portfolio People workshops*, who willingly shared their ideas, their fears and their hopes.

A particular word of thanks to my case histories who have opened up their 'portfolios' for inspection to show that it can be done – and done well.

Thanks to the Breakthrough Centre, where it all started, to Susanne and Roland for providing a beautiful and peaceful place to think and write and to Mole, my companion on contemplative walks by the River Dart.

A special acknowledgement must go to Elizabeth Hennessy and the crew at Random House for having the vision to publish this book.

A final 'thank you' to Jo, for keeping things ticking over while I ascended my writing tower, and without whose love, patience, encouragement and support this book could not have happened.

Foreword

'What do you do?'

Unless you are easily labelled as a doctor, an accountant, a social worker or a sagger-maker's bottom-knocker (as immortalised in the old TV quiz-show, 'What's My Line?'), this can be a tricky question.

Say you are a 'resting actor', a futures consultant like myself or a 'Portfolio Person' like Max Comfort, and you risk a sharp intake of breath and a glazed expression in reply. This can be quite off-putting for the examinee, who eventually learns to have what lawyers term 'further and better particulars' off pat.

As noted within, it was Professor Charles Handy, famed management guru, who first flagged up the concept of 'the Portfolio Career' in *The Future of Work* in 1984, consolidating it in *The Age of Unreason* in 1989. But it is not until now, as far as I know, that a whole book has been devoted to the subject in detail with its advantages and pitfalls, its do's and don'ts.

I wish I had had it at my bedside ever since I left the City 25 years ago ('What does Daddy do?' 'He fools about with other people's money', replies Emmeline, six), to go freelance. Since then, I too have been a portfolio person without knowing it – as an author, journalist, book-reviewer, lecturer, management consultant, futurist, school governor, charity trustee, psychotherapist and unofficial advisor to ageing cousins and aunts.

Whatever the money (and you may be surprised to hear that in a curious way, there is always just enough) this must be better than working for Microsoft, whose boss from hell, Bill Gates, says, 'you know, it's kinda romantic to sleep under your desk . . .'

If you agree in principle but are unsure in practice, take Comfort.

FRANCIS KINSMAN

Preface
What you can expect from this book

Portfolio People seeks to explain in very practical terms what it is like to be a Portfolio Person and to outline honestly the advantages and pitfalls for those who may be tempted to try a 'Portfolio Career'. It provides encouragement and advice for those pioneers already engaged in one. It is also a useful resource for those – managers or colleagues – who work with Portfolio People.

It begins in Part 1 with an overview of the chaos that is the world of work, how it arose, the demise of the traditional, post-Industrial Revolution job and the rise of Portfolio Working. There are examples of Portfolio People from around the world, since this is an international phenomenon.

In Part 2 it considers your situation: could you be a Portfolio Person? Would it serve you to try? Checklists and self-assessment exercises are provided. It sets out in some detail what you need to know and how to equip yourself for a Portfolio Career, in terms of materials and the support of other people.

Part 3 goes into detail over the complexities, problems and opportunities of running a Portfolio Career, both for those contemplating one and for those already in one. It discusses the four key areas that I have identified as being the most crucial for a Portfolio Person:

- time management;
- focus and commitment;
- trust;
- relationships.

It also gives some useful tips on financial controls and procedures.

Part 4 poses the question 'Where next?' both for you and everyone else, employed, unemployed, part-time, temporary, not yet employed, retired or retiring. Where do you want to be in a few years' time and what will be the quality of your life?

There are two ways you can make use of this book. You can simply read it or you can work with it. It's up to you and how much you want to get out of it, but I do hope you actually do the exercises and make the lists because I believe you will benefit enormously from them.

Even if you decide not to pursue a Portfolio Career, I hope you will enjoy this book since, as you will appreciate as you go through it, it covers more than just the mechanics and logistics of Portfolio Working.

Finally, a question, but please don't answer it until you've read the book. 'Why do you work?'

MAX COMFORT
Nappers Crossing, Devon, June 1996

Introduction

*To re-invent work in its fullest sense we need another word.
'Portfolio' might be that word. It is not, of course, a new word.
There are artists' portfolios, architects' portfolios, share portfolios.
A portfolio is a collection of different items, but a collection which
has a theme to it. The whole is greater than the parts. A share
portfolio has balance to it, mixing risk and security, income and
long-term gain in proper proportions, an artist's portfolio shows
how one talent has more than one way of displaying itself.*

*A work portfolio is a way of describing how the different bits of
work in our life fit together to form a balanced whole. 'Flat people'
as E M Forster called them, were those who had only one dimension
to their lives. He preferred rounded people. I would now call them
portfolio people . . .*

*Charles Handy, 'The Age of Unreason' published 1995 by Arrow
Books Limited*

HOW I ACQUIRED MY PORTFOLIO CAREER

It would have been great to start this book telling you that I became
a Portfolio Person by striking out and boldly going where no man
etc. That I had leapt defiantly off the highest ledges of my profession
in a moment of blind courage.

It *would* have been great.

But untrue.

The fact is, I didn't jump, I was pushed.

At the outset of the recession – I prefer to call it The 'Reality' – of
the early '90s, nobody in Britain wanted to build any more. In the
'80s, developers had filled our cities and towns with far too many,
largely unnecessary and speculative buildings. The Thatcher administration had encouraged us all into Never Never Land and most of
us were scrambling up the ramparts of Greed Castle. When the castle
collapsed under our collective weight, we were left with about seven

1

years over-supply of office space in London alone in 1991 and the housing market crashed, plunging the nation into an unwished for experience of instant karma.*

Naturally, in this climate of fear and uncertainty, very few people wanted to employ architects and planners like me. Like the buildings we had thrown up, there were now too many of us. And so I lost my job.

It was not an experience I'd care to repeat. That paralysing moment of truth, the day I was told I was no longer needed, I felt as though I had been exterminated. It was as if I was no longer a person, I had nothing to contribute and that, if I fell into a deep hole, no-one would ever notice I'd gone. To call it a living nightmare would not be an exaggeration, as those who have experienced redundancy or 'restructuring' – to quote a current euphemism – will know only too well.

So, there I was, cast adrift from a rapidly shrinking ship and wondering what on earth I could do to make a living.

To be honest, once I'd recovered my belief that the sun would really rise again in the morning, part of me was quite excited at the prospect – even relieved. Because, on occasion, I had experienced a worrying flash of doubt as I rushed from one important meeting to another or sat eating yet another expensively deconstructed fish over yet another power lunch. Might there be life outside those long, deep-carpeted, corporate corridors? Or after Sole Véronique? Was there perhaps something else, something I was missing, not seeing?

Of course everyone gets bored or dissatisfied with their lot at times – usually the morning after a particularly good dinner party or nocturnal nappy duty. The occasional day-dream is good for the soul, too. It may even be normal and healthy to glance over the edge occasionally while on Management Mountain at Bisneyland.

For me, however, that 'something else' had also to do with the niggling feeling that if all I did with my life was climb my particular glittering turret, Architecture, I would never get to see all of the

---

* Karma is best explained as a kind of multi-incarnational bank account. If you do kind things in one lifetime, you have a nice little nest egg of good deeds to stand you in good stead next time round. Do something bad and you get a whopping overdraft to pay off. There appears to be no way of telling exactly when you'll get the goodies or the bill and they can catch you unawares at any time over the next few hundred lifetimes. Instant karma is when the system decides not to wait for the odd aeon to pass by and presents you with the consequences of your actions immediately.

castle. Now, there are those who are happy and secure standing at their chosen battlements, watching the fast-moving events on the plain below. Despite being good at heights, I saw my professional ascent leading not to an expansion of my horizons but to a narrowing of them.

One thing I learnt working with a large architectural practice: you quickly develop a 'can do' attitude, particularly when wealthy clients come in at 5.30pm and ask you to design a multi-million pound shopping development (with a full set of scale drawings and coloured perspectives) for a board meeting at 10am the following morning. 'No problem,' my team would chorus in practised if weary unison, taking their cue from me, fixed grins already in place.

So, armed with a rather enlarged ego, a Filofax bulging with useful names and bags of optimism, I set out, Dick Whittington-like, to extract the 'mis' from misadventure.

THE CONTENTS OF MY PORTFOLIO

Gradually, with the help and encouragement of friends and contacts, I acquired a mixed lot of jobs and roles. I decorated people's bedrooms, I put up shelves, I cooked meals, I painted stage sets and I even wrote poetry for a living – well, it might have been a living if more people had wanted it but, in 'The Reality', iambic pentameters gave way to bulk-purchase fish fingers.

Gradually I built up a collection of assorted activities, some well paid, some not. Some not paid at all. At one point I had eight quite different income streams and a 'portfolio' of around ten occupations:

1 Closest to my 'old life', I did some project management. This usually had some connection with the built environment and often involved preparing clients for the realities of dealing with architects and the like.
2 I became an accredited DTI Business Planning Consultant and learnt that, despite Government assurances, clients don't actually want boring, inch-thick tomes that end up on the long, decorative bin on the wall (alias the bookshelf) but, rather, hands-on involvement and advice based on practical experience.
3 I was appointed part-time Development Manager and fund-raiser for the London Ecohouse – a proposed drop-in venue in

3

Hackney, East London with interactive demonstrations of sustainable lifestyles, basically promoting the idea of saving fuel, saving money and – by the by – saving the planet.

4 I helped to manage and co-ordinate the Breakthrough Centre* in West London, the world's only holistic business support club for the self-employed and terminally entrepreneurial where, in the words of its founder, Andrew Ferguson, 'you learn to work for yourself and *on* yourself'.

5 I also gave workshops at the Breakthrough Centre on Portfolio Working and ran something called the Max Comfort Masterclass which, like Paul Tortelier on TV, promoted the idea that you can learn both by participating and by watching others participate. I have developed what I call my inner voice (my intuition) during these workshops and, although it still surprises me with what it comes up with, it seems to work pretty well.

6 Someone whose business was in a parlous state told a friend of mine that he really needed 'someone I can burst into tears in front of'†. (The lawyers and the accountants weren't doing it for him.) My friend said: 'Max Comfort is your man.' There followed a wonderful business and personal relationship and the start of my Business Rescue Service, which has been going successfully ever since – that's to say: I haven't dropped one yet.

7 As people began to ask my advice on their relationships, their marriages and their experience of grief, I came to understand how intimately our emotional state is linked to our business performance. Applying these insights to immediate business situations produced a fascinating model for holistic 1:1 career counselling.

8 I became a facilitator, helping people and organisations to find and ground their vision, to reach a deeper and more effective understanding of their culture and then to implement and communicate the outcome more effectively.

9 All these activities, and more, are given free to individuals and organisations when the occasion demands. Other non-paying work in my portfolio includes being a trustee of

---

* The Breakthrough Centre is a holistic enterprise network. For information phone UK 01343 850303.
† (No, he didn't, as it happened, but he knew he could have done.)

4

charities concerned with sustainability, here in the UK and in the developing world.

10 My portfolio also includes a holistic massage qualification and at the time of writing I am in the middle of a five-year neo-Reichian psychotherapy training.

As housework is a fact of most people's working lives, I haven't included my supplementary duties in the home, although I thoroughly enjoy cooking and entertaining.

As you will have gathered, I have taken up book writing ...

To begin with, juggling this rather unwieldy assortment of activities, I felt a bit odd, rather unusual. At dinner parties, if asked what I did, I would hang my head rather shamefully and mutter into the *moules marinières*: 'Oh, this and that, you know.' My reputation as a doubtful dilettante, reinforced by the complete incomprehension of my fellow diners, hardened visibly. Concerned relatives would ask: 'When are you going to get a *proper* job?'

Then I discovered Handy. Professor Charles Handy and his amazing book: *The Age of Unreason**, in which he coined the phrase that was to legitimise my rag bag of roles: 'The Portfolio Career'. Suddenly, I was OK, a real person again. I was able to hold my head up with pride, quote Handy with complete assurance and not a little bravura and say: 'I'm a Portfolio Person, actually.'

* *The Age of Unreason* by Charles Handy, published 1990 by Arrow Books Limited.

PART ONE
WHAT IS A PORTFOLIO PERSON?

. . . the greatest human temptation is to settle for too little.

Thomas Merton, Trappist monk, mystic and writer.

Chapter One

The demise of the 'Job'

The world of work is turning itself inside out and upside down, shaking out the old conventions and expectations. Consequently there is now no such thing as a 'Job', in the permanent and secure sense that our parents and grandparents experienced it. This chapter looks at what the business gurus and others say will happen next.

Anyone in an environment that is not preparing him or her for a tougher future should move out fast.

John Kotter: 'The New Rules: How to Succeed in Today's Post-Corporate World', Free Press, 1995.

To prophesy is extremely difficult – especially with respect to the future.

Chinese proverb.

POKING AROUND IN THE MILLENNIUM SOUP

In 1918 my father started work in a London bank, straight from Grammar School. Some 50 years later he retired, from the same office in the same department of the same bank, a career interrupted only by his years in the RAF during World War II. When I started my architectural training in the '60s this kind of Job for Life was still common and, moreover, expected. Once I started working in architectural practices, I switched jobs like everyone else – partly out of necessity, partly to advance my career (and my overdraft facility) – but there was no question then of doing anything other than architecture.

Not only has all that changed in the last ten years but we don't *really* know yet what's going to replace our traditional ways of working or, indeed, how quickly these changes will catch up with us.

Most importantly, how they will affect us, change our way of being, even push us off our chosen life path and challenge our worldview and the dreams we're working so hard to reach.

Of course, there is no shortage of people telling us what we should be doing and forecasting our working futures for us. The pundits, gurus, experts and raconteurs have been having a field decade.

Hitherto staid business sections of seriously conservative newspapers are now regularly running headlines like 'Doing it for themselves – employers with vision and confidence are training staff to think for themselves', 'Plan for the future – personal development plans are essential', 'Get the right attitude', 'Skill diversity to prevent extinction – the survival of the fittest in the City requires a new level of multi-skilling', 'Making yourself totally indispensable on more than one level' or 'Love your work and take the pain out of life'. Pretty strong stuff for pages used to the 'Footsie 100', quarterly results and dividend forecasts.

Predictions are, inevitably, varied – but prediction, let's face it, is a hazardous business. In the '50s atomic power was going to bring free energy to everyone in the US; now they can't afford to run nuclear plants. In the mid '80s, *Fortune* magazine carried the prediction that, by the year 2010, North America would become the world's granary, the Pacific the world's manufacturing base and that Europe will become a discotheque. They could still be right.

John Naisbitt, on the other hand, writing in 1982 in *Megatrends*, accurately anticipated that the Information Society would replace the Industrial Society – years before the Internet had become a general phenomenon. He called too for a balance between 'the material wonders of technology' and 'the spiritual demands of our human nature' and advised that '. . . we are shifting from a managerial society to an entrepreneurial society.'*

Meanwhile, unusually, Charles Handy revisits the predictions he made in 1989 in *The Age of Unreason*† in his later book *The Empty Raincoat*.‡ He talks of the distress and confusion caused by the changes happening in our society and that he had not foreseen

---

* *Megatrends* by John Naisbitt, published in Warner Books Edition in 1984.
† *The Age of Unreason* by Charles Handy, published in 1995 by Arrow Books Ltd/Random House Group.
‡ *The Empty Raincoat* by Charles Handy, published in 1994 by Hutchinson/Random House UK Ltd.

the extent to which 'the opportunities for personal fulfilment which (he) had so confidently predicted would be complicated by the pressures of efficiency, that the new freedoms would often mean less equality and more misery, and that success might carry a disproportionate price.' He warns us against worshipping only at the feet of efficiency and sets out his principle of the inside-out doughnut, where the core represents the basic, common denominator activity or target and the space around the core represents '. . . our opportunity to make a difference, to live up to our full potential.'

Francis Kinsman wrote in 1990 that we are on a cusp between two ages, the Industrial Age and the dawning trans-Industrial Age and describes the 'Inner Directed' people who are its children, '. . . largely unconcerned about the opinion of them held by the world at large, since the criteria for their success and the norms for their behaviour are deep inside themselves.'*

In his book *Jobshift*, William Bridges brings us up to date, traces the demise of the job and considers the working patterns that are likely to replace it. The word 'job' as we now think of it had, before the Industrial Revolution, a quite different meaning: 'a particular task or undertaking, never . . . a role or position in an organisation.' For many, exchanging the relative independence of village livelihood for factory work was a demeaning experience and separated them from the means of supplying their own basic needs and those of their families; food could not now be grown – there was no time, no plot – it had to be bought instead.†

Now, says Bridges, the Job is being replaced by 'part-time and temporary work situations'. Since 'today's organisation is rapidly being transformed from a structure built out of jobs to a field of work needing to be done', it follows that '. . . jobs are rigid solutions to an elastic problem . . . and no longer socially adaptive creatures, and so they are going the way of the dinosaur.' To ram the point home he predicts that: 'To our counterparts at the end of the twenty-first century, today's struggle over (keeping and getting) jobs will seem like a fight over deck chairs on the Titanic.'

Matthew Fox pitches Work against Job and writes: 'Under the pressure of the world economic crunch that is creating a worldwide

* *Millennium* by Francis Kinsman, published in 1990 by W. H. Allen & Co.
† *Jobshift: How to Prosper in a Workplace Without Jobs* by William Bridges, published by Nicholas Brealey Publishing Ltd in 1994, 1995.

depression, the grave danger looms that we will seek only jobs – jobs at any price – and ignore the deeper questions of work such as how, why, and for whom we do our work.' He warns: 'We dare not miss the truly radical and creative moment in which we live – one in which we are being asked to redefine work itself', and continues: 'Work is an expression of the Spirit at work in the world through us. Work is that which puts us in touch with others, not so much at the level of personal interaction, but at the level of service in the community.'*

William DeFoore of the Dallas-based Institute for Personal and Professional Development refers to the traditional business phrases such as 'dog eat dog', 'shark' or 'cutthroat' and sees them as examples of the view that business is somehow immune from or above the normal requirements of morality in human behaviour. He says: 'The illusion of business as separate from humanity is similar to the idea of a head disconnected from its body. The body contains the heart and soul of our humanness, tied by survival needs to the planet itself. We hear this disconnection confirmed in the phrase "a good head for business". We recognise the absurdity of phrases like "a good heart for business" or "a good soul for business" in traditional business jargon. Despite these seeming absurdities, we need to reconnect our hearts, minds and bodies in our business relationships. Our very survival as a species may depend on it.'†

In his book *Small is Beautiful*, Schumacher calls for 'a proper philosophy of work which understands work not as that which it has become, an inhuman chore as soon as possible to be abolished by automation, but as something "decreed by Providence for the good of man's body and soul". Next to the family, it is work and the relationships established by work that are the true foundations of society.'‡

Just as my father was embarking on his life's career in 1918, Rudolf Steiner was writing *The Threefold Commonwealth*, a book that is only now receiving wider, serious attention. In it he outlines his theory of the triformation of the social organism and describes three distinct realms within it, each interacting with one another but

---

* *The Reinvention of Work* by Matthew Fox, published by HarperSan-Francisco in 1994.
† William DeFoore, writing in *New Leaders* magazine, January/February 1995.
‡ *Small is Beautiful* by E. F. Schumacher, published by Vintage in 1973.

to be treated autonomously: Liberty and the individual's spiritual and cultural rights, Equality and social and legal obligations and, finally, Fraternity as opposed to competition in the economic sector.*

INDUSTRIAL REVOLUTION, COMMUNICATIONS REVOLUTION – WHAT NEXT?

The references above are but a few examples of contemporary thinking on work and where it will – and won't – lead. There is, it seems to me, a common theme emerging from these observations, predictions and warnings: that of *integrality*. Today, modern science is discovering, through a growing and deepening understanding of our physical world, truths known for centuries to Eastern philosophers. The same opportunity for dynamic fusion is occurring in the millennial psyche of mankind. We are being given the chance to balance right and left brain, head and heart, need with want, to embrace Handy's 'doctrine of enough' in our lives as a first step to real personal freedom. The threads are there, ready to be woven together in a new pattern – if we choose:

- the break-up of the old system of closely defined jobs and the advent of 'work to be done' or tasking and co-operative team working;
- the 'flattening' of corporate structures and the need to develop a more entrepreneurial attitude and greater flexibility in our ways of working;
- the desire for more personal fulfilment and achieving our full potential as whole human beings;
- the growing appreciation that, contrary to Galbraithian doctrine, people *are* more important than goods and that, therefore, creative activity is more important than consumption;
- the integration of our spiritual principles in our work;
- the growing emergence and acceptance of the importance of EQ (emotional quotient) alongside the more familiar IQ;

* *Towards Social Renewal* by Rudolf Steiner, published by Rudolf Steiner Press in 1992. (Original German Edition, *Die Kernpunkte der Sozialen Frage in den Lebensnotwendigkeiten der Gegenwart und Zukunft*, 1919.)

- the integration of financial, ecological and social economics into a new 'Wholonomy' – a more whole Economy based on the original meaning of the word as 'stewardship' or the 'management of a household';
- the growing concept of the compatibility of 'service' with profit;
- the longing for real community, for ubiety or 'sense of place';
- the chance to belong and reflect, in a mobility-obsessed society with no time to stand still.

This list is not exhaustive, and we may not choose all of these threads – but some we will be *compelled* to weave into our working lives. The more threads we work with, the better the chance of producing something that serves us all; pick only a few and we may end up making a rope that snaps.

It is said that in the 21st century the new elite will consist of those with easy or quick access to information. I am not so sure, for having information is one thing, having the wisdom to use it is another. The Information Revolution is rapidly replacing the Industrial Revolution but the seeds of that transformation were already being sown as the old order reached its peak in the late '40s and have been quietly germinating all this time. Similarly now, in the midst of an era of seemingly limitless communication, at a time when facts, ideas and insights can circle the globe in an instant, I believe the next great revolution is already germinating. I would like to believe we are on the way to a Values Revolution, and the wise weaving of those new threads into a lasting, socially meaningful and beneficial tapestry.

There is no question that something is happening. Ironically, against a backdrop of redundancies and job reduction, there is a growing realisation that to be successful in business you have to honour the people working for you by giving them not only improved working conditions but a say in the business itself, a reason for being there which is more than a small buff envelope on Fridays. Allowing them to be an integral part of the *whole* process.

Among the many essential words now firmly implanted in required business vocabulary are 'empowerment' and 'devolution'. In some places business leaders are now doing rather more than just trying out these new buzz phrases for size at board meetings. They are actually implementing. And with spectacular results.

At ICI's works in Fayetteville, North Carolina, USA, the employees give the following reasons for the success of a recently implemented empowerment policy: they feel better about their work, they feel more involved, understand how the company works and have a new sense of pride in their jobs.

In Missouri, USA, Springfield Remanufacturing Inc., an organisation that reconditions old diesel engines, has introduced 'Open Book' management. Everything, including all financial detail, is explained to every one of the workers, right down to the guy who cleans the works toilets. The result is extraordinary: janitors have grasped the dynamics and workings of their business and some have become executives leading a successful expansion drive. Shop-floor workers feel they 'own' their business, their role takes on significance and importance in the greater scheme of things and they are suddenly taking an active and lively interest in the running of the company. The customers also feel and benefit from the change.

Not that breaking down the boundaries of the conventional Job is always a comfortable experience. As an architect I always felt more challenged by the prospect of designing a building for a large, greenfield site where – within reason – you had to make your own aesthetic rules. Building in town, where there were defined boundaries, rights of light to be respected and established reference points like historic 'neighbours' and old drains, was much easier. At Microsoft in Seattle there are no set working hours or job descriptions. The offices are always open, the lights always on. It's up to you how and when you achieve your task in your team, but that team will be watching your performance. Some people find this a liberating experience, others burn out.

The pressure to perform has not disappeared; it has simply moved from your line manager to your fellow team member. Increasingly, it will be generated by you. As a Portfolio Person, you may well stand a better chance than many of managing how you create and cope with that pressure.

In the next chapter we will look at the development of the Portfolio Career and its significance for tomorrow's world of working.

Chapter Summary

- The traditional 'job for life' is over.
- Corporate structures are breaking up and flattening.
- Everyone, particularly those in a full-time job, will need to become increasingly entrepreneurial.
- Work is becoming more about the quality of life and the

fulfilment it can deliver, less about its capacity to supply large amounts of money.

- Work is viewed by many as an opportunity for personal development, for creative activity, as a way of contributing to community.
- There is a growing awareness of the need for the integration of financial, social and environmental economics into a 'Wholonomy'.
- Service and stewardship are regarded by an increasing number of people as being as important as profit.
- When the Information Revolution has peaked in a few years' time, it will be replaced by a Values Revolution and the growing of skills necessary to use all the information wisely.
- Some organisations are discovering the intangible and tangible (bottom line) benefits of empowering their workforce, of giving them a purpose for working.

Chapter Two

The development of the Portfolio Career

The origins of Portfolio Working, the role of women, what's behind Portfolio Working and its role in the transformation of work.

> *'I feel as though I'm sitting on a volcano of creativity.'*
> *'I've simply got to take the lid off myself.'*
> *'It feels like being made redundant has given me the one chance in my life to do something really important.'*
> *'Now that I'm on my own, I need to find an effective way of using my skills for myself.'*
> *'Working for myself means I choose who I work with, not some invisible departmental head.'*

Participants at one Portfolio People workshop.

HISTORIC PORTFOLIO CAREERS

Although they may not have realised it, Portfolio People have been around for a long time. In some ways, a Portfolio Career is closer to the old task-orientated 'village' way of working and to the old notion of self-sufficiency. Although many people living in rural communities had a particular prime identifier such as thatcher or blacksmith, they were close to the source of their own sustenance, growing much of their own food, making most of their own work implements with their own hands or obtaining them from their near neighbours, bartering their surpluses. Most people performed a multitude of tasks, albeit in the context of a semi-feudal system, and so had to be multi-skilled – their lives depended on it. Flora Thompson's *Lark Rise to Candleford*, one of the best-known chronicles of this obsolete, late 19th Century lifestyle, describes the multi-tasked lives of simple folk in loving detail: the keeping, killing and curing of the family pig; the gleaning after harvest; the constant recycling of valuable clothes through the growing family; the tending of the allotment; the making of jam, jellies and wines; and the knowledge of herbs for their health, when only wealthy people called in the doctor.*

More recently, in World War II, many were obliged to take on other tasks (although, since the extra duties were often carried on at night, this is not a recommended role model). My mother had a very responsible day job in a bank, after which she would struggle home through cratered and rubble-strewn London streets, cook herself a simple meal on the one gas burner available and then change into her Air Raid Warden's uniform for a night of black-out checking.

WOMEN AND PORTFOLIO WORKING

It seems ironic that as more and more women successfully smash through the glass ceiling, the career structure itself is crumbling.

While it is dangerous to generalise, it does seem however as if women – perhaps better equipped by history and society for multi-tasking – adapt more successfully to part-time and Portfolio styles of working and indeed to change itself. Through the ages, working women have (without thinking about it, let alone labelling it) managed a 'Portfolio' of tasks. They have had to look after the needs of often large families, manage the household finances, act as the family 'therapist' and counsellor, look after animals, make and repair the family's clothes and maybe, in their 'spare' time, take a part-time job. This was often quite menial, cleaning, cooking, bar work, waiting or part-time factory work. Many were outworkers, often on low piece-rates.

(Little has changed, I can hear the women readers observe.)

Men, whose identity is traditionally more bound up with a single job, often suffer intensely if they are separated from it, for example through redundancy. Forcibly parted from their meaningful role, from being needed, from being part of a tribal group, many men may find themselves confronted by the terrifying question, 'Who the hell am I anyway?' without the female diversity of experience to supply alternative answers and a possible route out of the emotional nightmare.

* *Lark Rise to Candleford* by Flora Thompson, published in 1943 by Oxford University Press.

Of course, the phenomenon of full-time employment is most unlikely ever to disappear altogether. Nevertheless, with heightened anxiety about the full-time job-market, there is a growing instinct among workers to be proactive, effective, flexible and responsive in responding to new workstyles.

Part-time work and jobshare is indisputably on the up. In 1994, London's *Tonight* newspaper featured a report published by the GMB Union which reported that of some 68,300 new jobs created in London, less than 4,000 were full time.* Some six months later, reporting on an analysis of March 1995 employment figures in the UK, commissioned by the same Union, Anthony Bevins of *The Observer* newspaper concluded that '. . . more than three-quarters of the new jobs created since the start of last year's recovery are part-time', and that, in the final quarter of 1994, '. . . a total of 173,941 part-time jobs were created. At the same time, full-time jobs fell by 74,120, leaving a net position in new jobs of 99,825 – all of which are part-time.'†

In the same year, *FX* magazine reported that Sock Shop, the sock and fashion chain, with around 100 outlets, had decided to move most of its 400 staff to 20 hours a week over three days. Similarly, it reported that the major men's fashion chain the Burton Group had replaced 2,000 full-time staff with 3,000 part-timers.‡

In an article in *Management Today* in 1995, the Bamford Group concluded that '. . . the emerging work paradox is that in a post-job world, the only viable long-term career is to be a temp.' It cited a survey conducted by the Cranfield School of Management, showing that between 1989 and 1992, changing work patterns in the UK meant part-time working increased by 39%. It also gave figures for current company practice (1994) showing that 94% of companies were employing part-timers and 65% were using job sharers.§

It follows that, in order to survive, *people will increasingly have to take on more than one part-time job.*

John Naisbitt, author of *Megatrends* and *Megatrends Asia*, puts it even more strongly. He warns that if we in Europe don't end our

* 'Jobs are Part-time', *Tonight* newspaper, 21st September 1994.
† 'Part-time Boom Boosts Jobless Figures' by Anthony Bevins, *The Observer* newspaper, 19th March 1995.
‡ *FX* magazine, March 1994.
§ *Management Today* magazine, February 1995.

hostility to entrepreneurs (whom we badly need), it could mean that Europe will not be a 'growth player' in the future.*

The rationalising, downsizing, flattening and restructuring of the millennial corporate landscape is leaving a trail of fear, confusion and disorientation in its wake. Nevertheless, this business blitzkrieg also clears the ground for a thorough re-evaluation of work and why we do it – and history is joyously full of phoenixes and fresh starts.

We need to ask why it is that, despite 1960s predictions that, within twenty years, technological advances would enable most of us to spend two-thirds of our time in leisure pursuits, in fact the reverse is true? Why is it that with huge and growing numbers of 'reluctantly leisured' unemployed, people in employment often work far longer hours than before? Indeed the insecurity of the '90s has given rise to a new term, 'presenteeism', to describe those who consistently put in a 12+ hour day in a desperate effort to demonstrate their commitment and loyalty to the company and thus 'secure' their job.

SO WHAT'S REALLY BEHIND PORTFOLIO WORKING?

One very rewarding aspect of my new-found 'Portfolio Person' status was talking about my new career – and discovering a lot of people were doing exactly the same. In 1994, I started running workshops on Portfolio People in partnership with my colleague Gillian Edwards. The more workshops we ran, the more interest there was, not just from aspiring portfolio workers but from radio, television, magazines, professional bodies and other organisations. The concept of working at two or more quite separate jobs at the same time – Portfolio Working – had captured the national imagination.

We discovered a bank manager who also ran a restaurant, a solicitor who was also a photographer, a childrens' clothing company MD who was also a jobbing gardener, a director of a charity who also lectured in adult education when she wasn't organising large conferences, a health magazine columnist who managed the PR for a motoring organisation and composed and

* John Naisbitt's *Megatrends*, published in 1982 by Warner Books and *Megatrends Asia*, published in 1995 by Nicholas Brealey Publishing.

performed music and a papier mâché artist who is also an holistic massage practitioner.

We realised that a quiet revolution was happening in the workplace, that this was more than a few extroverts or misfits stitching together a patchwork career out of dire necessity or restlessness.

It was clearly part of a greater and more fundamental social phenomenon: the disintegration of traditional working cultures, the cracking of corporate structures and the breaking free of people tired of the shackles and limitations of the '9 to 5' routine, (or, in these days of job insecurity, more likely the '5 to 9' routine). So often in our workshops Gillian and I heard the complaint: 'I really enjoy my work but I don't want to have to do it five days a week. There are other things I want to do, other skills which I can't use in this job.'

This transformation in attitudes to work, while still in its infancy, is spurred on by the growing anxiety over job security. At Portfolio People workshops I give for executives, there is always a strong motivation to prepare for the perceived imminent demise of the traditional job. The participants know they are only temporarily secure and, because forewarned is forearmed (and because they for the most part recognise themselves to be highly marketable), they are not going to hang around waiting for the situation to catch up with them.

These people are very determined that, in return for facing challenging change, their quality of life should improve significantly, that there should be an expansion of life experience and that levels of work-related stress should be effectively reduced. Many studies reinforce the perception that there is not necessarily a correlation between increased salary and increased quality of living. Indeed it can be sobering to count the cost of a rise in wages, and correspondent rise in responsibility, in terms of personal fulfilment, relationships with colleagues and friends, significant time with family and the opportunity to use other talents and skills than those employed in the course of 'the job'.

Put simply, people are asking: 'What are we working for?'

This question (and it is a fundamental one) is a reflection of our innate need to be more than just a job, one role, someone else's label; our need to have purpose in our lives, to allow more of our abilities and interests to be engaged in the process of work and to do what we do for more than a wage.

It is interesting that many employees today are being encouraged to develop Personal Development Plans (PDPs), to counter the erosion of the traditional career path and to increase their chances of survival and advancement in a radically changing corporate culture. They are increasingly being encouraged to see themselves as entrepreneurs within their company, to develop more 'edge' and supply their competencies as a commodity to the organisation.

It is not hard to appreciate the enormous stress that this shift in the working environment puts on employees at all levels. Described by psychologists as 'the silent killer of the '90s', stress at work is claimed by 70% of office workers to be the leading source of problems in their lives, according to statistics currently available, and is held to be responsible for a lowered resistance to illness, sleep deprivation and a cause of injuries and accidents at work.

A large number of books on stress management tend to reinforce the view of worker as 'victim', tackling the symptoms but ignoring the root cause of disempowerment. In the UK, for example, it is now possible to get free eye-care from your employer if you work at a VDU, but there is no legislation curtailing the amount of time employees spend at a screen.

Part of the stress of traditional work can be the sheer difficulty of getting to it. With congested roads and overcrowded public transportation systems, commuting is becoming a worsening night-mare. A recent study estimated that, by 2001, everyone in the UK would spend on average two weeks a year sitting in a traffic jam.

In view of our growing mobility crisis, it isn't surprising that home-working is on the increase – some believe it will be adopted by 25% of the UK's working population by the end of the decade. Telecommunications companies are already targeting home-workers in their marketing. Magazines and support organisations have sprung up to service the growing band who choose the flexibility of working at home where, as one person put it, at least they can load the washing machine between phone calls and sit at their desk in their pyjamas.

PORTFOLIO PEOPLE: A SIGNIFICANT GROUP

At this volatile and anxious period in the history of the job, when many of the old certainties and boundaries are being pushed over, Portfolio People are pioneering a new attitude of independence and self-reliance. Whether or not they are aware of it, they are

22

developing the skill-sets and free-flow work-style that tomorrow's work environment demands, along with the necessary curiosity, flexibility and versatility to make them a valuable free-floating part of many organisations.

Since they don't rely on one income stream, but can call on several, they are often more alert and confident and, therefore, more attractive to the 'freelance' employers who are their clients.

Finally, unlike others in more traditional working environments, Portfolio People have the opportunity to create a framework to grow themselves as they grow their businesses, to develop a self-awareness from which a wisdom can develop, the wisdom necessary for the coming Values Revolution.

In that they may indeed represent the majority work mode of the future, Portfolio People are a group to watch.

Chapter Summary

- Portfolio working is closer to the old, pre-Industrial Revolution way of working, with its numerous tasks and rôles, with few single-activity Jobs and when people were more self-sufficient in providing their material needs.
- Most women have always had a Portfolio Career and one that has largely gone unnoticed and unacknowledged.
- Since the advent of the 'job', men have identified strongly with it and have often suffered a crisis of identity when it came to an end through redundancy or retirement.
- The number of part-time jobs has increased significantly over the last decade.
- Experts confidently predict that 'temping' is the only viable long-term career.
- People will need to take more than one part-time job.
- Portfolio Working is capturing people's imaginations.
- People are increasingly asking: 'What am I working for?'
- Stress, particularly at work, is the silent killer of the '90s.
- Homeworking is on the increase and becoming accepted and promoted.
- Portfolio People are pioneering the skills and attitudes necessary to both survive and enjoy work in the next century.
- Portfolio People, with their independence and confidence, are attractive people to work with and have working for you.

Chapter Three

Portfolio People – personal stories

Examples of people from different parts of the world who have chosen a Portfolio Career, the reasons for their choice and how well – or not so well – it served them.

Q: *'Why did you become a Portfolio Person?'*

A: *'To be self-employed and fully self-expressed. It struck me as more "natural" and creative than being a full time employee in one job.'*

A: *'I wanted my working life to be varied and exciting – also to be nose to nose with my personal growth while at the same time fully exploring my creative skills for profit.'*

A: *'Life was so boring in my five day a week, eight hours a day job. The same tasks, the same office, the same people, the same conversations, the same jokes, the same awful coffee – I just knew so clearly that if I didn't get out and engage with my life, it would simply go on by without me.'*

A: *'I had to do something after I was made redundant – restructuring they called it (very amusing!) – so I looked around for things that I could do to pay the home loan and the food bills and, after a period of intense terror, discovered I rather liked this crazy way of working. Now, having tasted freedom, wild horses wouldn't drag me back to ****** plc.'*

I asked a number of friends who are dedicated Portfolio People to honestly describe their careers, how they came to them and how they experience the realities of this particular workstyle. The stories below represent a wide range of backgrounds and, particularly, a variety of Portfolio Careers, each reflecting different good and not so good aspects of this way of working.

The first story comes from Russia, a country in massive transformation, yet one where the survival tactics necessary during

24

Soviet years have metamorphosed into a 'can-do' attitude to rival that of the US. They have entrepreneurs – *predprinimateli* – like you've never heard of.

Lena Sokolova, Sosnovy Bor, near St Petersburg, Russia

I studied for 10 years at one of the so-called 'English schools'. These are considered very good in Russia with some subjects being taught in English, so that when I finished the school I had a good basis for entering University or College. At the same time I had also studied at Music School and Art School. I entered the (then) Leningrad Architectural & Building Academy and graduated as an architect six years later. My first job was at the State Design firm as an architect.

I always had a lot of hobbies. One of them, wickerwork, attracted me so much that I decided to set up a special course to teach people and so I became a teacher. Later my husband (an architect too) and I started our private architectural practice. (I was not prevented from combining my duties at the State firm with running our own private practice.) As we couldn't afford an accountant (it would be very expensive) I had to do this job myself. When my children went to school I left my job at the State Design firm and became a school teacher.

Now I teach History of Art, Drawing and Modelling at a private school and look after the accounts at my husband's private architectural practice. I've also just taken the World Bank course on Economy and this allows me to carry out valuations for a number of real estate and investment projects. This is a job with excellent prospects in Russia as there are not many such specialists in the country at the moment and they'll be more and more in demand in the future. Since the essential basis for that speciality is a knowledge of architecture and accountancy, I can use my experience to good effect.

I think I could never have just one job because I need freedom. In fact I do what I want to do and I love a portfolio way of working, it's a way of life and thinking. I could never live in a different way, it just wouldn't be of interest for me. Nor has making a lot of money been my motivation. When I went to look at schools I had two motivations:

a) I wanted to be near my children and the salary from working at the school went on their education; and

b) *I believed that nobody could give my children an Art education better than I could.*

I think that the good aspects of my portfolio way of working are the feeling of independence, self-sufficiency and – above all – freedom.

The not so good aspects of my portfolio way of working are that this lifestyle is a real problem for my family. I can't spend a lot of time on my husband and children and it feels sometimes as though I live mainly for my pleasure.

Lena Sokolova, Sosnovy Bor, 1st June 1996.

Peter Settelen, London, UK

Peter's story illustrates the same openness to explore new ways of working but his activities stem more clearly from one source – acting. He came to prominence for his speech work with Princess Diana.

I trained as an actor at the London Academy of Music and Dramatic Art and then worked extensively in TV with occasional forays into the theatre.

I remember being told that an actor's training would be brilliant for people who never became actors. Now, more than 20 years later, I realise what they meant.

Having shifted from my prime focus of acting, which was the only job I'd ever had or thought I wanted, a whole host of other possibilities opened up for me. When asked to describe what I do, I feel as though I'm showing off or perhaps sounding desperate to impress, as I reel off my list. I'm an actor, director, book, screen- and speech-writer and communications consultant. I'm also a husband and parent.

My first step out of the limitations I'd placed on myself came when I was waiting for something wonderful to happen – as actors do. I received a call from a friend, a newscaster with 'Sky News' who asked me if I knew someone who could help a friend of hers who desperately wanted to be a newscaster but who had, at that time, a very squeaky, high-pitched voice. I said I'd try to think of someone but maybe I'd help her myself. 'Give me a few days to think about it', I said. Two days later, I got a call from the Head of 'Sky News', asking me if I could meet him to discuss the possibility of training around 30 of his reporters whom he felt could do with a little help with their 'on air' delivery.

There was one small problem: I had no plans to teach. Nevertheless, I went to meet him and walked out 90 minutes later, having agreed to start the following week. I returned home to think about what I was going to do with them. Like driving a car, I'd forgotten how I did what I did. I realised that all my knowledge and experience could have a different use, a different value, which I'd never considered. I'd opened a door which was to lead me into areas I could never have imagined.

A client at Sky recommended me to a friend of hers who was a fitness trainer. She wanted me to help her talk in front of people. I ended up directing her in her fitness videos. A client of hers happened to be the Princess of Wales who asked me if I would help her with her speeches. I ended up writing them as well. Lunch with her resulted in me being doorstepped by 30 journalists. I ended up on the front page of every tabloid newspaper. This led to me being approached by a publisher who asked me to write a book on my methods. While writing the book, Just Talk to Me*, a feature film idea started to grow in my head. I'm now writing that film.*

You may ask where the husband and father come in. What I do to earn my living and how I live my life are inextricably linked. Much of what I do in my personal life affects what I do professionally and vice versa. All are interconnected, all nurturing and feeding both me and my family.

All came out of what I thought was only one skill. Yet my chosen profession contained within it all the elements of the rest. We all have untapped potentials. I know, as I continue to open my door even wider, that there are potentials waiting to happen. I wonder what they are?

Peter Settelen, London, 24th June 1996.

Gillian Edwards

Gillian and I worked together at the Breakthrough Centre and other venues, giving Portfolio People workshops and letting our participants know how this workstyle was for us. I experience Gillian as an

* *Just Talk to Me* by Peter Settelen, published in 1995 by Thorsons.

unrivalled networker, a tremendous connector of people with people, people with opportunities, opportunities with opportunities. In many ways, her infectious enthusiasm and positivity have taken her beyond the 'can do' to a point where it's no longer a question of 'possibly', more a case of 'definitely'.

Gillian's story began conventionally in a Quaker girls' boarding school, from where she went to university. It was there that things started to go 'wrong'. She left her degree course through a failed relationship and thus began her quest for meaning and success in her life. In the course of her search for her role in the world and in order to survive, she did many different jobs and experienced numerous setbacks. She trained as a drama teacher and then found that she hated teaching in schools. She taught English as a foreign language, acted occasionally, drove for the pop group Pink Floyd, was a PA for a lawyer and a vacuum cleaner salesperson.

At one point she devised a scheme for a centre in the South of France which offered support for single mothers and their children. This failed. So did renewed attempts to teach English as a foreign language in the UK and in Italy. It was as if she had all the skills but could never find a situation where they could blossom. So she started asking for help and, as had always been the case, friends began to make connections for her. Her enthusiasm, marketing abilities and teaching skills were recognised by an American educationalist who had established the New Learning Centre in London, offering teaching for children abandoned by conventional education as being 'too difficult' and guidance for their parents.

Having long forsworn teaching, she found herself loving it. She had arrived at last at the place that matched, honoured and encouraged her particular abilities. As her work at the centre was initially part-time, she added other part-time activities to this, all needing the enthusiasm and vitality that Gillian brings to everything she does. At one time she had five different jobs, one for every day of the week, as the UK's *Daily Telegraph* headlined in April 1994, including teaching, lecturing, giving workshops, administration, marketing and acting. Significantly, she kept Thursdays free as a maintenance day, a time for personal and domestic matters and a time for herself.

Gradually, some of the jobs came to an end but the time thus released was needed by the New Learning Centre as it expanded. Now, although she still keeps at least a day free for 'maintenance', much of her energy is devoted to this centre. Gillian exemplifies a

Portfolio Person who, through much adversity, has found a way of working which supports her own personal values; she works with people who share those values, she is a master of time management, she has the ability to focus at any given time on the task in hand rather than worry about the next one, she actively and successfully trusts herself and others and, although she is not a high earner, she would not change what she does even if guaranteed a fortune. Above all, Gillian sees little separation between work and life. In fact, she sees them as one. Gillian's job is being – being Gillian.

Nicholas Orosz, Bristol, UK

Nicholas also started out on the accepted route to success but found himself constrained by the demands of that success, prevented from doing many of the things that nourished him and unable to be himself for most of his waking hours. Having taken what, at the time, seemed an enormous risk, his personal values and his highly professional approach to what he does are now freed from a conventional context and allowed to range freely through all his interests, paying and non-paying.

I read Law at Cambridge, qualified as a solicitor and worked in London and in Paris for over 10 years, specialising in mergers, acquisitions, venture capital, domestic banking, international finance and privatisations.

Initially, the work was interesting, often exciting and intellectually stimulating. However, I increasingly found my career extremely frustrating. I had little inclination to play office politics. My outside interests were both varied and quite alternative and were an important part of me. I did not reveal much of my true self or my aspirations in the office mainly because I felt they would be misunderstood and, frankly, it would not have been a good career move to do so. The overwhelming pressure of work and the relentlessly long hours meant that I could by no means lead a balanced life. I was regularly in the office from 8am to 9pm and taking work home at weekends. Working through the night was by no means unusual. The main problem was the unpredictability of the hours. I lost all my vitality and joie de vivre. All I knew was that I wanted my life back.

I had many diverse interests which I wanted to pursue but did not know how. I knew instinctively that I needed to work for myself in a way where nobody could buy my time for 36 hours (let alone the 80 I actually worked) a week and where I could control my own agenda. The transition over a two-year period was hard, full of doubts and fears about financial security, but was made possible by establishing a business in Network Marketing, distributing a range of Aloe Vera healing products, from which I now derive a satisfactory and ever-increasing passive income. This has given me a degree of financial independence and I have an extremely flexible working pattern. Whilst this is by no means vocational, it is an outstanding vehicle for me to schedule my time to do other things which I love and find creative.

I now have time to devote to being a trustee of two charities, whose work I passionately care about. One is working for Tibetan refugees in India and the other is a meditation centre in Devon. Additionally, I have developed my Fine Art Photography, I regularly exhibit my work and have had some of it published. I intend to publish a book of my photographs with accompanying prose and poetry.

Paradoxically, now that I am away from full time law, the lawyer within me has found expression in the area of human rights. I co-edited a book entitled 'Tibet: the Position in International Law' and I am now considering other opportunities to use my legal skills in this field on a part-time basis.

I love the flexibility of my new lifestyle. To be able to have an effective day in my office at home and listen to the Test Match commentary on the radio is very satisfying. The one area which I do now find quite difficult is that of discipline and I find, ironically, that I do need to instil more structure into my days.

My life as an employee now seems like a bad dream. I miss nothing of that life. My life has changed beyond all recognition – it is now fuller, more satisfying, balanced and creative. I have more time for myself, my personal growth, my home life and I am far happier that I am able to spend time doing what I love and feel passionate about.

Nicholas Orosz, Bristol, UK, 29th June 1996.

Veronica Needa, London, UK

Veronica combines enormous enthusiasm, curiosity and a great love of people and fuels it with amazing reserves of energy. Her

30

multicultural upbringing has led her to explore beyond the boundaries others stay within and to a rich life filled increasingly with recognition and appreciation for her many talents.

Born of Eurasian parents and English, Chinese, Japanese and French-Syrian grandparents, I grew up in Hong Kong, straddling British and Chinese worlds, a toe-hold in both and not quite sure where I was standing in the middle of it all. My mum wanted me to grow up with as much of the advantages of a little English girl as she could create for me in Hong Kong, so she put me through the English school system there.

The first time I ever left Hong Kong was to come to England to go to University. I chose Nottingham because the picture of the campus in their prospectus looked good. I left with a BSc (Hons) in Psychology, having spent an intercalated year with the Work Research Unit in the Department of Employment, who were pioneering job redesign and restructuring of the work place. I spent my time trailing organisational consultants up and down the country as we worked with unions and management to find ways of improving the quality of working life.

However, having completed my degree, I had to put all this behind me, return to Hong Kong to look after my sick father and to support the family business – a flower shop. I grew up in this shop, helping in all ways, from unpacking and arranging the flowers to taking orders, Interflora and bookkeeping. It was a social drop-in centre for all our friends and I knew who wanted tea, who preferred coffee, with/ without sugar/milk and so on. When my father died, mum and I kept the business going and I took evening classes at the Hong Kong University in Chinese Language and History and Jungian Psychology and became busily involved in amateur dramatics.

When mum and I sold the business we both 'retired' and I wondered what to do with myself. I taught English as a second language part-time for the British Council for a year. Teaching was fun and I was about to go for a qualification in TOEFL when I fell into the theatrical profession – by accident. I went to a performance by the Chung Ying Theatre Company and was struck to the core with a deep longing and knew then that this was what I wanted to be part of. It took me months to pluck up courage and knock on the door of their administrator to offer my help. I was truly just volunteering my time and energy to support something I believed in. I said I was inventive, good with my hands, bilingual, enthusiastic and had a driving licence. They were interviewing for stage management at the time and were desperate to engage at least one person who could drive. Since none of their applicants could, I was offered a full-time job as a Deputy Stage Manager. Thus followed two very fulfilling years of doing meaningful creative work impacting on the community and in an ensemble atmosphere.

I left Chung Ying and came back to the UK to train in Acting and Drama at the Bristol Old Vic Theatre School really because I now needed to perform on stage, not just behind the scenes. I got an Equity Card within weeks of leaving Bristol and since then I have always been self-employed.

Working as an actress is a very intermittent activity. Part and parcel of the profession is uncertainty. Not knowing what's next. This has never daunted me. And I have never felt single-minded about acting as a career. It is one of the many things I do very well. Fortunately, my identity is not locked into it.

During my first years as an actress in the UK, gaining wide-ranging experience in professional theatre work and doing further short trainings in additional performing skills, I also worked as a builder's apprentice, receptionist in a law firm, gardener, seamstress and theatre designer's assistant. Gradually I became involved with community and young people's theatre work and eventually found my métier in Playback Theatre, became a Director of London Playback Theatre, a Board member of the International Playback Theatre Network and now teach and perform this improvisational, therapeutic theatre worldwide.

I am a founding member of Yellow Earth Theatre, a co-operative of British East-Asian theatre practitioners, producing theatre that comes out of our cross-cultural experience. As a storyteller of Chinese myths, legends and folk-tales I have worked in schools on behalf of the Commonwealth Institute, Chinese Community Centres and at the Victoria & Albert Museum. As an inventor and designer I have made models of golf courses, created patio gardens and am currently involved in designing and decorating six flats to be let out by a property development company run by a friend.

Being a Portfolio Person is my natural way of being and I was doing it long before it had a name and credibility. Since coming to the UK I have only ever had either regular part-time work, short-term full time contracts, one-off session work or project work done in my own time. A lot of the work I do (administration, fundraising, publicity and public relations) is not immediately paid for but gives *me rewards in all sorts of other ways and often creates paid work in the future.*

My parents always wanted me to be 'happy' and do whatever I wanted. So much freedom was a boon and a bane. They never pushed or shoved me in any direction, so I drifted and took opportunities as they came to me. They gave me the feeling that I would always be taken care of so I have grown up with their financial cushion and also with the deep-seated feeling that my needs would always be met. At an unconscious level I have always 'trusted the universe' and 'followed my vision'. I am much more conscious of this now and practise it with more awareness. 'Living on purpose' is the basis of my portfolio lifestyle.

If I could change the way I work it would be in the areas of focus and time management. I tend to be a workaholic and to say yes to doing things that I am interested in without checking to see if I can really fit everything into the 24 hours of a day. So in the past I have had periods of burn-out and I have had to stay in bed doing nothing for at least a week. A big lesson that I need to learn is how to make time for myself to do nothing. My work is my life expression and I have blurred the edges between work and play. This is my next step: disentangling my work time from my play time. I love my work, I am passionate about what I do in all its different and creative manifestations, but I know the work will 'breathe' more easily and sit better and more productively with me when I find a good way to contain it and leave clear space around it all.

Veronica Needa, London, UK, 9th July 1996.

Robert Wallis, London, UK

Robert has had an unusual mixture of activities in his portfolio but demonstrates the effectiveness of having one 'base' activity to which can be added others as and when they appear or are created. This is also emphasised by his conscious decision to 'drop' some of the 'jobs' he has been doing in order to take more time for himself.

After attaining a Diploma in Accountancy, I qualified as a chartered accountant and worked for a London law firm, learning about the hard edge of business in their insolvency and liquidations depart-ment. Although originally groomed to take over the family fashion business, this was sold and I became the first franchisee of Tie Rack plc, building a chain of shops which was turning over £3m within four years. I am now owner of 'Off the Cuff', a menswear accessories company with shops in central London and Gatwick Airport.

I became a Portfolio Person as a way to feed my different motivations in a relatively structured way since I had so many varied and unrelated interests. Just making the decision to take Fridays off from the menswear business was humungous! I had a huge bin of unfulfilled aspirations buried in my own waste-paper basket so I began to focus more introspectively. Consequently I qualified as a psychosynthesis* practitioner and started a practice from my home one day and two evenings per week.

I worked as a volunteer in the Marie Curie Hospice for the terminally ill, starting with helping out with serving drinks and providing company and ending up forming a Friday meditation and relaxation group for residents and carers, family and friends and, with the help of friends who were musicians, setting up reminiscence groups based around music. These were incredibly popular but it was hard, heart-breaking work, seeing the joy in their faces, their hearts opening and the sadness in their lives passing. Here, in the company of all types of people from all walks of life, young, elderly, road workers and convicted psychopaths, I learned to be 'Present' with people with very little future.

I was involved in setting up a youth project called WYSE which organises summer camps for 18–28 year olds from all over the world who have a vision for their community or, in some way, a life of service. The project is very successful and the camps have become truly international in flavour with venues as far flung as Sweden and Argentina. Combining our unique skills, my partner and I have started a new venture, 'Touch Down', offering de-stressing products and related services to those experiencing the fast pace of life in the city.

In theory, a portfolio career is very flexible way of working, but it is open to becoming overextended and its 'downside' can be doing lots of little things without necessarily doing anything particularly well or fully because there is always somewhere else to go or something else to focus on.

* A transpersonal and humanistic branch of psychotherapy, founded by Robert Asagioli, a contemporary of Freud and Jung.

My portfolio career has changed with my needs and circumstances. I have temporarily exchanged my therapy practice and my hospice work for developing my singing and musical abilities. This is a better balance for my life right now with the demands of business and personal life and I have used the space created for travel and fun, particularly exploring drawing, painting and my love of dancing. Writing this has brought home to me that on balance I have much to be thankful for working in this way. Over the past years my aim has been to simplify my life and learn to cope with burn-out from over activity. I am realising that, with more unscheduled gaps in my life, it's not what I do that's important but the way I do it and my attitude to this. In this context my unrealistic expectations of wanting to change the world in a big, dramatic way have given way to the realisation that little changes seem to stick more. Due to its flexibility, my portfolio career seems to allow these more modest changes to occur organically.

Robert Wallis, London, UK, 30th July 1996.

Norliah Karim, Selangor, Malaysia

Norliah also has a family business as a base and has used this security to explore all her abilities and develop a portfolio of activities that will sustain her emotionally and materially for years to come.

I am married with one son and am a Director of PGN Noradli Sdn Bhd, my family's Computer Stationery business. After an education at St George's Girls School and the University of Science, Malaysia, where I got an Honours Degree in Social Science, I joined ABN Bank, working first in Penang and then Kuala Lumpur as Personnel Officer, Credit Officer and Credit Manager. In 1985 I was appointed Branch Manager of Southern Bank and at the same time established the Nor Management Centre which managed small businesses, wrote working papers for them, made loan applications on behalf of small business operators and offered consulting services. This business I am building in parallel with other positions and projects.

I left Southern Bank in 1989 to become an HR Consultant in Organisational Development with SMPD Management Consultants and in 1996 became a Director of DAC Management Consultancy

Sdn Bhd with responsibility for human resources, training and organisation development.

The strategy behind my portfolio career is the building up of a business track record over the next ten years so that when I retire I will have a flourishing business to come to. I love the flexibility and freedom of being on my own, the feeling that I don't need to bend to the will of superiors and having ample time for myself to do as I please and for my child.

I am actively looking for ways to improve my marketing skills and would very much like to enter into partnerships with other specialists. I would also like to create a more regular income!

Norliah Abdul Karim, Selangor, 10th July 1996.

Julie Lacy, Melbourne, Australia

Julie's story illustrates the difficulties of uprooting a carefully constructed Portfolio Career to a new location and the time needed for building up a new one. It also graphically illustrates how easy it is to be tipped almost imperceptibly over the line that divides enthusiasm from exhaustion, from being to being overworked.

April 16th 1989 – arrival Heathrow, London 3am following a twelve hour emergency stopover in Dhahran owing to a reported bomb aboard my flight from Bangkok. In January 1995 I departed from London in the same state that I arrived – exhausted – leaving behind what had become my new home, my struggle, my love and my Portfolio life.

I didn't know it had a name. I was doing what I could to survive – financially, artistically, emotionally, spiritually. When I discovered that this crazy, over-committed, wonderfully challenging and perpetually draining lifestyle was becoming fashionable, I had a sense that I was, rather than suffering from a deviation of Multiple Personality Disorder, part of a growing movement. To be sure, moving – at least geographically – is inherent to the Portfolio world, in my case from Ladbroke Grove to Fulham, Kensington, Corringham (Essex) and Grendon Underwood (Buckinghamshire). And one needs an inner momentum – both a desire and an ability to move one's head around the differing demands of each activity. Wearing different hats – I tend to think wardrobe (shapeless dresses for Grendon Prison, funky

36

*leggings for Performers Dance College) and having sufficient 'fuel'
to propel oneself from one scene to the next.*

*At the height (or is that the breadth?) of my Portfolio Career I
was engaged in the following:*

Day	Place	Activity
Monday	Charing Cross Hospital	• Attending Ward Round of Inpatient Mental Health Unit
	Fulham	• Inpatient Mental Health Unit
		• Conducting Analytic Group Outpatient Unit
Tuesday	Performers Dance College	• Teaching Drama
Wednesday	Performers Dance College	• Teaching Drama
Thursday	Inner London Schools	• Supply Teaching
Friday	HM Prison, Grendon	• Directing Psychodrama Groups
Saturday	Home	• Sleep
		• Portobello Market
		• Friends
Sunday	St Clements & St James Community Centre	• London Playback Theatre* rehearsal and/or business meeting

In addition to this weekly schedule, I did the following:

*monthly Playback Theatre performances at Kings Cross;
monthly Weekend Training Seminars in Holland Park;
monthly Supervision sessions for Psychodrama in Tufnell Park;
monthly Supervision sessions for Group Analytic Group in Fulham;
twice weekly Group therapy and supervision sessions;
fortnightly Psychodrama sessions in private practice.*

*I used to have what I called my '7-eleven days' – leave home at
7am and return at 11pm. As Artistic Director of London Playback,
my private phone line was also the company business line so I would
come home to seventeen messages and – while running a bath – be
thinking about the clinical session not written up, the phone bill not
paid, the seminar reading not read, the dance students' reports not
written . . .*

*My final nine months in London were a countdown toward the end
– I was on reserve tank. Driving home from Grendon Prison on a
jammed M4 motorway in freezing fog at 7pm Friday night, having
attended two Wing Community meetings, directed two psychodrama*

---

* Playback Theatre enacts personal stories brought by members of its
audience.

groups and given two feedback sessions to staff, I would play George Duke's 'Brazilian Love Affair' and picture myself dancing on the beach in the sun.

Why? I am what my mother calls a 'people person'. I thrive and flow in and amongst groups of people – actors, colleagues, clients, students . . . Certainly those last few years in London were too much. My health suffered. They were also filled with the greatest joy, rewards, pain, beauty, love, learning, soul and creative gifts. Eighteen months later I feel the loss still.

The success of those years relied on God's grace, my initiative, my clients, my trainers, my colleagues all combining to support and enhance my portfolio work.

Melbourne in July is cold and grey. I'm not a portfolio person now. I'm unemployed, poor, frustrated, sad. There are no clients, no theatre company, no colleagues. I'm starting again. It's tough. Bits and bobs here and there. Good feedback – no consistency. I trust it will change – or I will. A Portfolio Person is a bit of a chameleon. Natural Selection will sort me out – or an Angel will point me in the right direction. Perhaps I should get on another aeroplane – without the drama of a bomb – a gentle landing, a different web to weave.

Julie Lacy, Rippon Lea, Melbourne, Australia, 16th July 1996.

Note:
Julie's most recent work has been conducting workshops in schools on the issues of bullying and the prevention of sexual abuse. She has also created TarotDrama, a unique blending of psychodrama and the Tarot where the personal and collective unconscious come into play.

Adam Glasser

What is interesting about Adam's story is the problem of conflicting activities in the portfolio and the emotional polarisation that affects his way of dealing with this.

Having always worked self-employed from home, my 'portfolio' consists of two main strands: the most important is music – playing keyboards and harmonica, gigging, teaching, composing, arranging and running a band. Several years ago I decided to try and give up some of the less rewarding music work (functions and commercial gigs) and replace the income with an activity other than music. I have always had a deep knowledge of continental cycling so I decided to exploit that, beginning a second career as a journalist writing specialist features for cycling magazines.

The cycling work started to take off when I wrote two treatments for bike documentaries and was employed as an associate producer. However, this interfered with my musical objectives and after a year of very good earning, I gave up the TV work and concentrated on writing for a few specialist publications. My inexperience at the beginning was a real handicap and caused me to take an inordinate amount of time to write the features, but thankfully this has changed.

The problem with my portfolio existence is that the one activity often disrupts the other. My attention feels split between two disparate working lives. To be really successful at both jobs would require a very disciplined approach. This is possible but I am still struggling to achieve it. When in a stressed or pessimistic phase I am tempted to give up writing in order to concentrate more on music, but enjoy the writing and need the income. Optimistic good sense tells me to persevere with being a Portfolio Person.

Adam Glasser, London, UK, 31st July 1996.

I hope the stories above illustrate both the good and not so good aspects of having a Portfolio Career. For me they all point to the need to exercise careful control over the number of activities we Portfolio People get involved in through our enthusiasm or 'can do' attitude. They underline, as well, the importance of taking time for oneself, of putting enough energy into one or two activities that will sustain other, non-income-creating pursuits, pursuits which, in turn, will emotionally sustain the money creating activities. It is also clear that being open to involvement in non-earning tasks, because they are fun or worthwhile, can lead to income generation. This is the multi-symbiotic nature of Portfolio Working: each activity contributes to the whole but needs the support of all the others. What is also apparent is the differing degree in which working and living become enmeshed in Portfolio Careers, and that some people feel this close relationship as a threat while others experience it as a joy. Finally I am struck by the way these people have so often uncovered a cache of abilities inside just one skill and also by the way they have multiplied their earning and fulfilment capacities by focusing on their attitudes and values as well as on their skills and know-how.

PART TWO
SO YOU WANT TO BE A
PORTFOLIO PERSON?

What you need to know about being a Portfolio Person in terms of practicalities and the tangibles like mobile phones and keeping a cashflow projection going. Also, what to watch out for in terms of the intangibles: fear, courage, cheek and curiosity.

Until one is committed, there is hesitancy, the chance to draw back, always ineffectiveness. Concerning all acts of initiative (and creation) there is one elementary truth, the ignorance of which kills countless ideas and splendid plans: that the moment one definitely commits oneself, then Providence moves too. All sorts of things occur to help one that would never otherwise have occurred. A whole stream of events issues from the decision, raising in one's favour all manner of unforeseen incidents and meetings and material assistance, which no man could have dreamed would have come his way.

'The Scottish Himalayan Expedition' by W. H. Murray.

Whatever you can do,
or dream you can, begin it.
Boldness has genius,
power and magic in it.

Goethe

Chapter Four

Could You Do it?

This chapter gives you the opportunity to check how you *feel* about being a Portfolio Person. You may end up convinced either way . . .

'Our deepest fear is not that we are inadequate. Our deepest fear is that we are powerful beyond measure. It is our light, not our darkness, that most frightens us. We ask ourselves: "Who am I to be brilliant, gorgeous, talented, fabulous?" Actually, who are you not to be? You are a child of God. Your playing small doesn't serve the world. There's nothing enlightened about shrinking so that other people won't feel insecure around you. We are all meant to shine; we unconsciously give other people permission to do the same. As we are liberated from our own fear, our presence automatically liberates others.'

Nelson Mandela in his inaugural address as President of South Africa, 1994.

'Take the Adventure, heed the call, now ere the irrevocable moment passes! 'Tis but a banging of the door behind you, a blithesome step forward, and you are out of the old life and into the new!'

Sea Rat in 'The Wind in the Willows' by Kenneth Grahame.

WHAT IT'S LIKE TO HAVE A PORTFOLIO CAREER

Having operated a Portfolio Career for some time now, I occasionally reflect on how different it is from those times in the past when I've been self-employed but working with one client or with one client at a time. Perhaps because I always had lots of other things going on as well, so-called 'outside interests' that didn't actually bring in an income but which nevertheless occupied my mind, it doesn't feel tremendously different. Where it does differ from my previous bouts of freelancing is in its increased complexity. More of my activities are now being paid for and therefore have that added professional edge – and a cranked-up level of tension.

Nowadays, my Portfolio is more modest than before. I am actively trying to focus on fewer activities and to simplify my lifestyle. Despite the financial uncertainty (and this is hardly any worse than for those with 'proper' jobs these days) and the difficulties of time planning, it would have to be a very unusual 'job', with a lot of autonomy, to attract me back into one income stream and full-time employment.

Why?

Because, for one thing, I have never experienced boredom since I started out on my Portfolio Career. There simply isn't time. And there's almost no repetitive work. My natural curiosity is not frustrated as I am free to explore and test myself in other areas of work. My working life is full of variety, everything I do I really enjoy since I don't have to do any of it all the time. As a consequence, I come fresh and enthusiastic to just about everything I do.

Moreover, knowledge and insights gained in one activity can be used in another. I am constantly cross-networking my own experience to great effect and I can offer my clients a large and ever-growing basket of skills and competencies. They can see this and also sense, albeit unconsciously, my independence from, and objectivity towards, their agenda.

I can say too, for the first time in my working life, that I feel all right about *everything* I do. There were times in my architectural career when I was considerably less than happy with the projects I was responsible for. I worried sometimes about the ethics of building what Prince Charles called 'mirror-glassed stumps' in our historic centres or the commercial, environmental and social implications for the nearby towns and villages of planning yet another out-of-town shopping development on a hitherto peaceful greenfield site. Yet, 'trapped' in my job, there was little I could do – except leave.

Despite sometimes crazy deadlines, my work is no longer work in the sense, as Meister Eckhart put it, that I am 'being worked instead of working' – except when I choose. I would be the first to admit that there is a temptation to do too much and that I don't always get my time management right, but at least it's my choice, not someone else's.

Above all, working for oneself, particularly in a Portfolio Career, is more than earning a living. I have found that it is also, and increasingly, a very potent vehicle for self-development. You are confronted by yourself, comforted by yourself, monitored by yourself and, occasionally, praised by yourself. Your path to self-knowledge is accelerated – indeed, it can sometimes feel like being on a gymnasium walking machine without an 'off' switch. Since understanding oneself better can lead to understanding others better, it follows that, as with the always-bubbling stockpot on the kitchen stove, you can add this into a skills mix which grows richer and richer over time.

I don't want to give the impression that Portfolio Working is the easiest, best or only way to work. It isn't easy, nor does it suit everyone. On the other hand, I doubt that it's more stressful than some full-time jobs. And it can be cyclical. My colleague Gillian Edwards, at one time billed by the tabloid press as 'The Woman with a Job for every Day of the Week', now has one job which occupies all her working time. This happened quite naturally and she loves what she is doing. However, I know that the experience of being a Portfolio Person stands her in good stead as she has carried with her the habit of cross-networking her skills and life experiences – to her own and everyone else's advantage.

SO, COULD YOU BE A PORTFOLIO PERSON?

Could you be a Portfolio Person?

To answer this question, you need to start by looking at where you are right now and to then review your personal vision for yourself. To do that, you'll need to:

- create a quiet space for yourself
- have a pad and pen handy.

THE SEVEN-HOUR ITCH

We talk of the seven-year itch. What about the seven-hour itch? Do you itch to get to work? Or do you itch for something else while you're there?

Are you content, happy or excited by what you do to earn a living between the magic hours of 9am and 5pm? *Are* they magic hours?

Does what you do get you out of bed? In time? Does it reach parts of you that no other occupation can reach?

If the answer to all or most of these is 'yes', 'pretty much' or even 'most of the time', that's great. You're probably best staying with what you've got while keeping a weather-eye out for the accumulating cumuli of change.

If the answer is: 'not in the slightest', perhaps you are ready for a change, to try something different, to widen your horizons. With the best will in the world, it's possible to get fed up with a good job, however well you do it and despite any amount of positive feedback. As you go through life, learning more about yourself and others, you're constantly changing; the job may not be. If you've reached the point in your organisation where it feels as if it no longer has anything meaty to offer you, you may have simply outgrown it. You've worked hard to reach your boredom threshold. Now it's just a matter of time as to who recognises this first – you or the boss.

You may be seething where you are now, having to put up with someone in your up line making a total mess of a task you could do far better.

Even if you're climbing the ladder in the organisation – as opposed to sliding down the snake – it's possible that you could become a victim of that strange game that's played in the traditional work environment: promotion out of your comfort zone. You know how it goes: somebody is really good at doing what they do and the powers that be want to reward them, to show appreciation. (And to ensure that they stay doing it for this company and not the competition.) They can't pay them above their grade income band. That would upset a lot of people who rely on their salary as a measure of their worth and their success. So, the only way that can be found to reward this energy and ability is to promote the person from where they're happy, feeling needed and fulfilled, to a completely unfamiliar position, often with little or no training. ('You'll soon get the hang of it!') Here, they can no longer do so much of what they were happy doing well and, worst of all, they may have to watch others doing it badly.

Or maybe those cumuli have already descended over your place of work and turned into a fog of uncertainty, fear and confusion with rumours of redundancies, cuts and that unkindest of euphemisms: restructuring. Maybe it's time to go. Perhaps those rumours have become reality and you're facing redundancy or the fact that your contract is not going to be renewed.

You may not even have started your career yet. There you are, straining every muscle, concentrating hard, eyes down on that achievement track, intent on winning the Great Job Race. But, between breaths, you may be worrying that, by the time you get anywhere near the tape, those two white lines will have vanished, the crowd gone home and the marshals left with the prizes for another arena.

Or perhaps you are fed up with the 'dog eat dog' atmosphere and demeaning conditions at your current place of work and are desperate to set up your own company where you can instil your personal values in all areas of the business.

It's possible you've got a hobby that could be turned into a means of making money or an idea for a thingummy that's been niggling away in your head for a while; the thingummy that, one day, is going to make your fortune. Has that day come?

You may simply be feeling that there must be more to work than this. This daily and rather irrelevant routine that seems not to be serving anyone, the world or – in particular – you. Perhaps you are suffering from a condition I call 'divine discontent'. I'm sorry, but it's terminal.

Stop for a moment and consider if and where you fit into these scenarios. Are they familiar? Do they touch a nerve? Do you *have* an itch – particularly between 9am and 5pm?

Let's see . . .

THE SEVEN-HOUR ITCH EXERCISE

Please write down on your pad what it is you do for a living, using a matrix like the one below:

For those of you who currently have one job, don't just use one word or phrase like 'Architect', 'Nurse' or 'IT Manager'. Break down your activities into sub activities. For example, as an architect, I got to do:

- conceptual work;
- technical research;
- presentations;
- negotiations with bureaucracy;
- meetings with clients and colleagues;

THE 7 HOUR ITCH EXERCISE				
Activity/Job	Overall Fulfilment	Effort Involved	Reward	Total

- administration;
- writing/checking contracts;
- liasing/co-ordinating different disciplines;
- meetings with contractors and sub-contractors;
- site inspections;
- paperwork etc;
- making models.

For those of you who are already Portfolio Working, list your different jobs and break them down as above.

Now, on a scale of 1 to 10, rate how you *feel* about what you do in terms of:

- Overall fulfilment – not income, but how good or excited you feel when you think about your job or career. You should include praise and appreciation from colleagues. For example you could rate it as follows:
    1 = it really doesn't do anything for me, it's dull and boring or its pointless and I hate it; to
    10 = I love being at the office/studio/workshop.

- Effort involved – not physical effort but how much of a chore it *feels* like when you're getting out of bed to go to your work. You could rate it something like this:

    1 = it's a real struggle to get up for work in the morning; to
    10 = it's like falling off a log.

- Reward – not actual figures but whether you honestly *feel* you get a reasonable income from your work relative to others and relative to your financial needs (no, I don't mean a Maserati!):

    1 = I get paid a pittance for what I do; to
    10 = I get paid really well for what I do and I feel acknowledged.

If you have one job, you can either give one overall 'reward' rating or, if you feel comfortable doing it this way, individually rate the different activities. For example, as an civil engineer, do you *feel* you are adequately compensated for the time spent up to your knees in mud-filled holes or working your way through that rash of yellow post-it notes that's miraculously appeared on your desk while you were out?

If you have more than one job, rate them separately but break them down as well.

Now add up the totals for the three columns, *horizontally*.

- Any jobs or parts of a job that scored 25 or more: you're doing pretty well.
- 20+: OK but maybe check out the low scores again.
- 15+: You need to look hard at what you do.
- 10+: There could well be a crisis looming.
- Less than 10: *What* did you say you did?

Now add up the totals for each of the three columns, *vertically*. Then divide the answer by the number of entries in that column. For example, if the total in your Overall Fulfilment column is 102 and you have 17 entries in it, the result will be 6. This represents an average.

- An average of 8 or more is brilliant. You star!
- 7 is pretty good.
- 6 is OK but could be better.

- 5 is not good, you need to have a serious chat with yourself.
- 4 and below is awful. Time to dust off your re-thinking cap.

How did you score?

More importantly, how do you feel having done the exercise? Do you view your job or jobs any differently? If you don't, that's fine.

If you do, write on your pad now what it is that's changed in your attitude.

OK? Now for some envisioning...

THE SEVEN-YEAR VISION

Vision?

Yes, I do mean vision. We all have some kind of an idea of what, in an ideal world, we'd like to be doing, who we'd like to be doing it with, where we'd like to be doing it and what sort of person we'd be as a result.

For some of us it is as simple and undefined as a vague longing for something better, something other than the sheer drudge or unpleasantness of our current situation. The feeling that if only we could find it, there would be, should be ... that something again.

Then, again, some of us are surrounded by the material manifestations of our efforts so far, our lives seem arranged, sorted and settled. Things are good. Yet...? We are sometimes bored, stifled, unfulfilled, feeling stuck in that comfortable rut – and boredom, surprising as it may seem, is stressful.

Others have a plan or a sense of direction. It might be buying a bigger, better house, getting a degree, going round the world, marrying the person we love, achieving recognition in our chosen field, finding a really satisfying occupation or, simply, feeling better about ourselves and who we are. We may well be rather driven by our plans for ourselves, a bit fanatical, sometimes so sharply focused that we become blinkered and obsessed, sparing no thought for others – or ourselves – in our striving for our goals.

Where do you fit in this visionary panorama? Do you have a well-defined life programme or just occasional divine dermatitis?

Here's how to find out:

- Do the visualisation below. Either record it – leaving pauses as indicated – and play it back to yourself, or get a friend to read it out to you – again with the pauses.

(By the way, if you've never done anything like this before and you think you might feel a bit 'stupid' sitting fantasising with your eyes closed to some 'New Age' mumbo-jumbo, don't worry. Everyone feels the same way when they start. Think of it as a guided daydream. Anyway, who's going to know? And it *is* very effective.)
Just before you start . . .
Here are some I pulled out of my bag of visions:

- building my own house;
- working with more businesses;
- getting my portfolio down to more manageable proportions;
- taking more time for me;
- seeing more of the world before it shrinks too much;
- making a modest income from writing;
- getting to know myself better.

Now you have a go . . .

VISIONS EXERCISE

- Make sure you are somewhere peaceful and comfortable and that any potential interruptions are dealt with – phone off the hook, no-one expected to call for a while, dog watered and in its basket etc. If you like, play some soothing *orchestral* music very quietly in the background.
- Now switch on your tape or start your friend with the reading.

Here goes . . .

- 'Close your eyes.'
  [Pause for 5 seconds]

- 'Take a deep breath.'
  [Pause for a deep breath]

- 'Make your hands into fists, clench them tight and hold for a count of three.'

[Pause for 5 seconds]

- 'Slowly unclench your hands and stretch your fingers out as far as they'll go.'
  [Pause for 10 seconds]
- 'Imagine that you can now go anywhere in the world you like. Anywhere. There are no restrictions, no practical difficulties, no limitations. No expense spared. If what you want is to be on a beach in Fiji wearing a grass skirt, that's fine. If you want to be climbing in the Himalaya, you can. If you long to be on the track at Le Mans in a Ferrari Testosterone, go for it. Take your time to find somewhere that really inspires you. The only rule is that it has to be your very own perfect place, unique to you, there only for you. The only other rule is that you give your imagination complete freedom. No-one but you is experiencing this flight into your fantasy, so enjoy the privacy and the power.'
  [Pause for 20 seconds]
- 'Picture in your mind whether you are sitting, lying or standing. On a rock, a beach or a mountain top. Feel the hardness of the stone, the softness of the sand, the lushness of the deep grass or the majesty of the peak.'
  [Pause for 10 seconds]
- 'How does it feel to be in this place you've chosen? Peaceful, exhilarating, thrilling, scary? Check out how you are feeling right now in your special place.'
  [Pause for 10 seconds]
- 'Is the sun shining where you are? If so, is it high in the sky or just rising? Picture it in your mind and see if you can feel its warmth on your face, on your head or on your arms.'
  [Pause for 10 seconds]
- 'What can you hear in this special place of yours? Imagine the sounds that are there – birds, sea, the wind in the trees, a waterfall perhaps. Other people – laughing, talking excitedly, singing? What sounds are there?'
  [Pause for 15 seconds]
- 'Is it warm where you are – or cold? Is there a breeze or a gale or is the air quite still? Are you wearing many clothes to keep you warm or are you scantily clad in the heat?'
  [Pause for 15 seconds]
- 'Look carefully at your surroundings. Are you in a mountainous

place, high above the valley or deep in a jungle with huge trees towering over you? Or are you perhaps on a huge rolling plain. Notice in your mind's eye the shape of the hills, the colour of the mountains or sea, the line of the far horizon.'

[Pause for 15 seconds]

- 'Now consider what you are doing here, in this perfect place of yours. Are you a traveller, an explorer, are you working here or building something? Why have you come here? What is your purpose?'

[Pause for 15 seconds]

- 'Now notice if anyone is with you or are you completely alone? If you have company, is it someone you know, someone you love, someone you're scared of?'

[Pause for 10 seconds]

- 'If you are alone, is there someone you would like to spirit over to join you? Now is your chance to bring them here, to your side.'

[Pause for 10 seconds]

- 'This someone who is with you, what are they saying? Are they being gentle, funny, loving? How do you feel about what they are saying?'

[Pause for 10 seconds]

- 'What would you like to say to them?'

[Pause for 15 seconds]

- 'How do they feel about what you are saying?'

[Pause for 15 seconds]

- 'Now picture this person slowly walking away, away into a great golden light. They beckon and you follow. You experience the light permeating every part of you.'

[Pause for 10 seconds]

- 'Feel it soaking into you, cleansing and refreshing.'

[Pause for 10 seconds]

- 'As the light begins to fade, choose a place in which to keep hold of a small piece of it, a secure place that you can revisit when you want to experience the light again, to rekindle it. It could be somewhere inside of you or it could be outside, like the palm of your hand. Choose carefully.'

[Pause for 20 seconds]

- 'Now experience how your body is feeling. Is it heavy, or tingling? Light or glowing? Stay with the feeling for a few moments.'

VISIONS LIST				
Visions	Impossible	Crazy	Exciting & Inspiring	Total

[Pause for 30 seconds]
- 'Now, when you are ready, slowly open your eyes and stretch your arms wide.'

[Pause for 10 seconds]
- 'Thank you.'

Well, how was that? How do you feel now? Relaxed, excited, frustrated, angry, embarrassed? Whatever you are feeling is fine. Please note it down in your pad.

YOUR VISIONS LIST

Now that you've done the visualisation, write down on your pad at least ten things you'd like to do in your life – or qualities you'd like to have in it. If you have more than ten, that's great. We'll call it your Visions List. Please set it out in the form of the matrix above.

Now, in the first column, called 'Impossible', put in a number on a scale of 1 to 10 how utterly impossible it is to achieve this particular vision. For example, if it's about as likely to happen as water flowing upstream, give it a 1; on the other hand, if it does have a significant degree of reality, despite certain practicalities to be ironed out, give it 10.

In the second column, called 'Crazy', rate the vision on a scale of 1 to 10 on how totally and ridiculously daft it is. If it's merely fairly unusual, the sort of thing you might not immediately tell your mother-in-law, give it a 1. However, if it's so crazy you daren't tell your very best best friend, give it a 10.

In the third column, called 'Exciting and Inspiring', rate the vision on a scale of 1 to 10 according to how thrilled and charged up you are by it. The more charged you are, the higher the rating.

Now, as before, do your maths and add the columns *horizontally*.

A vision with a score of 25+ is great – what are you waiting for? Ring it in bright, visionary purple!

20+ is pretty good too. Mark it for serious attention.

15+ is OK but don't spend too much time on it.

10+ put this one on a back burner.

10– put this one out in the darkest corner of the wood shed.

OK.

- Please take a break. This visioning business is more energy draining than you may think.

How well does what you do now for a living fit with the list you've just written? Please note your response on your pad.

HOW WEALTHY ARE YOU?

Now we've considered where you'd like to be, let's consider where you are, right now.

When you did your Vision List, did you include those things in your vision which don't necessarily make money but which come under the heading of 'Abundance'?

If not, please go back and put them in.

Here's a little reminder about Abundance. It's important to make this distinction: Abundance is *not* a product of having money; money is one of the many products of being abundant. As Andrew

Ferguson says in his book *Creating Abundance*, 'There is never enough money or prosperity to create abundance. We know this. We have tried it. We in the West have created and accumulated vast wealth, and all it has generated is the fear of losing it and a desire for even more wealth, more conquests and more growth at the expense of others.'* Simply, if we focus only on money for attaining our desired quality of life, we'll never reach it. Or we'll be so busy making money to achieve our goals that we'll fail to notice life slipping ever faster by – until too late. How many people do you know who are in that particular trap? I thought so.

I experience Abundance as being more about quality than quantity It can be as simple as a lover's smile or a walk in a springtime wood; it can be as complex as a brilliant moment of insight after hours of careful study or a secret let out at last to explain and complete a puzzling aspect of one's life. It can mean things turning up at exactly the right moment, unexpectedly.

Yes, of course it's easier to enjoy your children in a lovely, large, sunny garden than in a small, shadowed yard – but I remember having just as wonderful, warm family moments in a cramped caravan as in a huge house.

Now back to your pad again.

ABUNDANCE EXERCISE

On a fresh page, please list all the good things in your life. Yes, even that!

For example, you might include:

- being fit and healthy;
- your intelligence;
- your memories;
- a loving partner;
- smashing children;
- supportive and non-critical parents;
- a nice house in a beautiful area;
- a fast car;

* *Creating Abundance* by Andrew Ferguson, published in 1992 by Judy Piatkus (Publishers) Limited.

- a reasonable income.

Okay. Now you do it.

Thank you.

Now put a tick against those that you can experience without the need of money. Interesting, isn't it?

Now you've done the Abundance Exercise, ring those items on your list that most nearly – or exactly – equate to some of the items on your Visions List. What did you get? Are there some things or qualities you already have or nearly have in your life that you'd maybe forgotten about?

If there are, note them down.

If there are not, that's fine too.

Now we've looked at the good things in your life, let's look at your talents.

HOW GIFTED ARE YOU?

This is intended to be a process of discovery, not self criticism. Very few of us are endowed with genius but most of us are pretty good at quite a few things. The world of business would be a much saner – and safer – place if there were fewer budding Supermen and Wonderwomen whirling around.

So what are your resources? How long since you got that imaginary portfolio down off the wardrobe, dusted it off and checked the contents? Since that excruciating session with the careers teacher? Or when you'd finished your training and weren't sure whether heavy engineering was really you?

Let's have a look now.

This time, we'll skip the ubiquitous list and do a map instead. You may need to get some coloured markers and a large piece of paper to pin on the wall.

YOUR SKILLS AND INTERESTS MAP

Starting with your childhood, write up all the things you've done in your life so far. I don't mean: 'Got up, had breakfast, went to bed.' We've all done our fair share of that. No. More like the sports you played, the hobbies you had – yes, even trainspotting – and the societies you joined while at college or university. And all the activities, interests and jobs since. Everything. It doesn't matter where you put them on the sheet, the more scattered the better.

Bear in mind that this is *not* meant to be a list of things you might be able to turn into paid work. It is meant to jog your memory of the things you enjoyed doing and were good at, to remind you of your diversity, however remote this may seem from paying the bills. If you once mixed a mean dry Martini or grew huge chrysanthemums include that too.

Nor is it intended to convince anyone of anything. So, if you didn't *really* single-handedly transform the entire Accounts Department of Megacorp Inc. – which is what you'd maybe like a prospective employer to read into your resumé – don't worry about that here; you are the only person who'll see it, so you can be honest – or modest.

Now see if you can find connections between some of your skills and interests. For example, I would probably connect taking clocks apart as a child with designing the construction details of a complex roof, linking the two with a line and a phrase like 'a desire to know how things really work'. Or an early ability for active listening with my counselling work. Much of it is very straightforward, but consider how often we fail to see the obvious, that which is right in our face.

How did you get on? Did you surprise yourself with the number of things you've done? If you feel there isn't very much or you can't remember everything, leave it for a while and come back to it.

Now I'd like you to carry out a SWOT analysis. WOT? No, nothing to do with flies, but everything to do with your Strengths, Weaknesses, Opportunities and Threats. Remember, no one else is going to see this either so you can be completely up front with yourself. On the other hand, you *could* elicit some feedback from friends and family who you can trust to reflect your good and not so good points, fairly and without frills. (If you can't stomach that idea, try reflecting on what your friends and family *might* say about you. Go on, let your imagination rip.) Keep notes.

Then dig out those testimonials, thank you letters and evaluations. In the privacy of your own mind, check your feelings against each of them. Were they fair, accurate or downright biased? More notes please!

YOUR PERSONAL SWOT ANALYSIS

Try to put down at least 10 points in each category.

First, please list your Strengths, in terms of character, skills and experience. For example, you may be resolute in times of crisis, able to fix computers and know all about drilling for oil in the Indian Ocean.

Now list your Weaknesses. This is more difficult, but do your best. I don't wish to imply anything, so these are just examples. Perhaps you don't speak up soon enough when you perceive an awkward situation developing, maybe you're lousy at accounts and possibly you don't have much experience of working a database.

Next come Opportunities. These could be people you know who are excellent contacts, actual or developing situations – niches – (in your present work context or outside it) which might benefit from some of your input, or openings to develop and hone your existing skills base.

Finally, Threats. These could be the imminent demise of your job, the presence of predatory competition around a project you've worked hard to grow or the possible collapse of the market for your skills and experience.

What you've done so far is open up the possibilities a bit and broaden your appreciation and understanding of yourself. If you are already a Portfolio Person, you may have found the exercises above amusing or even instructive.

Let's pause for a moment to take stock. Are you still feeling curious or enthusiastic about the concept of a Portfolio Career? If you are, great. If not, it would be a good idea to write down what feelings you now have about the subject and how they differ from the feelings when you first picked up this book.

It could be that it all seems too complicated or, more likely if you are in a full-time job right now, too risky.

I'd like to deal with that now.

RUNNING THE RISK OF RELEASE, SPRINGBOARDS AND DOVETAILS

So often I've heard the refrain: 'I hate my job so much I'd like to blow up the office, but I can't possibly leave now, there's nothing concrete to replace it with. I can't see any way out and I can't bear to stay. I'm completely stuck.' The fear and hatred some people feel toward their present situation is so all-consuming, the focus so narrow, that anything else is excluded. There is no way they will entertain even the possibility of an alternative, let alone a vision.

The way out of it is simple and surprising: to really appreciate that hateful job for what it is – a blessing, a resource and a potential springboard. When I tell people this they look at me as if I'm mad. Then I explain: blessing because it brings them to a potential pivotal point in their lives and shows them where, what or how they don't want to be doing; resource because, whatever they may say, it is providing material support and, finally – and this is the biggest surprise – springboard, because it can continue to provide support while they look around for their next step. If they can take their energy out of hatred and resentment and put it into appreciation, the future becomes viable.

If you are feeling stuck in your work situation, try this: it's another visualisation, you'll get used to them.

Remember the basic rules: peaceful space, no interruptions. And to record it yourself or have a friend read it to you, in either case keeping the pauses in.

- Now switch on your tape or start your friend with the reading. Here goes . . .

- 'Close your eyes.'
  [Pause for 5 seconds]
- 'Take a deep breath.'
  [Pause for a deep breath]
- 'Make your hands into fists, clench them tight and hold for a count of three.'
  [Pause for 5 seconds]
- 'Slowly unclench your hands and stretch your fingers out as far as they'll go.'
  [Pause for 10 seconds]
- 'Picture yourself in a situation at work that you hate. Get in as much detail as possible. See your desk, the paraphernalia, the piles of files, the PC, the three half-empty coffee mugs, the abundant waste bin.'
  [Pause for 15 seconds]
- 'Now become aware of the immediate surroundings. See the

colour of the carpet, the arrangement of the furniture, note the sounds, smell the smells.'

[Pause for 15 seconds]

- 'Widen your vision to include the whole floor. Notice the Fire Exit, the coffee machine (the hot chocolate's still empty), the photocopier and stores cupboard. Is your line manager's door open or closed?'

[Pause for 15 seconds]

- 'Now imagine yourself gently lifting above the floor, floating effortlessly through the ceiling, through the hallowed Directors' Suite, up and out until you are right over the building and its surroundings.'

[Pause for 15 seconds]

- 'Still you move, high above the ground, and the building becomes tiny and insignificant, gradually melding in with all the other buildings until you can no longer distinguish it from the rest.'

[Pause for 20 seconds]

- 'The group of buildings shrinks even further until it becomes like a splash of colours on a map, greys and reds and browns on a green landscape. Observe how form gives way increasingly to colour as the town or city where you work slowly disappears.'

[Pause for 25 seconds]

- 'You are floating above it all, detached from it – yet aware. Explore that feeling of detachment and the wider perspective you are now enjoying.'

[Pause for 20 seconds]

- 'Enjoy the sensation of being so high, so removed from the everyday and then allow yourself to gently fall, back to the town where you work.'

[Pause for 15 seconds]

- 'As the buildings and other features of the town become visible, the parks and green spaces, the river, greet them as you would familiar friends after a journey.'

[Pause for 15 seconds]

- 'As you re-enter your place of work, notice how everything is the same. Everything, except perhaps you. Have you changed? Do you feel a little different now? Or has the place changed too?'

[Pause for 20 seconds]

- 'Experience the feeling you have as you slip back into your workspace. Recognise it, if you can, as somewhere you'll be occupying for a little while longer, somewhere that, for all its drawbacks, supports you for the moment.'

[Pause for 20 seconds]

- 'Now experience how your body is feeling. Is it heavy, or tingling? Light or glowing? Stay with the feeling for a few moments.'

[Pause for 30 seconds]

- 'Now, when you are ready, slowly open your eyes and stretch your arms wide.'

[Pause for 10 seconds]

- 'Thank you.'

Well, how was that? How do you feel now? Relaxed, excited, frustrated, angry, embarrassed? Whatever you are feeling is fine. Please note it down in your pad.

I'm often struck by the number of young people, barely into employment, who complain that they don't want to – let's see – teach English, be a lawyer or write advertising copy all their lives. Realistically, it's unlikely that they will stay very long with what they are doing in its present form, if at all, but they are often so focused in their fear and misery that they can't see beyond next week. In comes the springboard syndrome, and life begins to look brighter.

With a springboard, it's possible to dovetail the present with the future, gradually shifting your energy from one to the other. As you begin to prepare for your next role, you'll feel an increased sense of purpose and direction, you'll experience the beginning of the end of the present situation and this will reduce the amount of effort you put into hating it. You may even come to really appreciate the role that your present job has in supporting your transition and – yes – enjoy it, particularly now that it's finite.

How long you give yourself to make this transition will depend on a number of factors: your desperation, outside opportunities, how well placed you are to take advantage of them, your financial commitments and responsibilities, your family situation and so on.

So my advice is nearly always not to leap off that corporate ledge but to use the windowsills and drainpipes as handholds for a planned descent to ground level. Then you can start turning your vision for yourself into practical reality.

It hardly needs pointing out that the other important aspect of dovetailing is that you can test the new situation to a degree without completely blowing it with the present one. Of course there's a risk that you might not re-enter the corporate edifice through the same window or even on the same floor, but there's less chance of going splat!

Being made redundant with a sum of money in the bank is an extreme but very lucky form of dovetailing. I'm not saying it's easy – I've been there and had the pain – but it does mean you're supported while you look around for the next step.

Let's look at an example of dovetailing.

John worked in the Production Department of a large and established publishing company and had always felt he could improve on some of the designs he had to look after, that there was a creative part of him just bursting to 'have a go'. He invested in an evening design course and discovered he really enjoyed it. This completed, he negotiated a four-day week with his company. As they were keen to retain him and his specialist production skills, they agreed.

At first he had to adjust to a lower salary and to the novel sensation of working at home, but he invested in a state of the art graphics kit for his computer and began doing odd design jobs for friends and colleagues. He found that his intimate knowledge of production gave him an edge over other designers and that many of the traditional misunderstandings and problems simply didn't occur when he was in charge. His growing client base found the same.

The time came when he could no longer justify working every evening and every weekend as well as his one day on top of his 'day job' as something was bound to suffer sooner or later – almost certainly him. So he had to choose between putting the brakes on his growing independent business or leaving his old job. He chose the latter but first negotiated a retained consultancy with his old firm based on his particular knowledge of the production process. This served him, with a regular income based on good, commercial day rates, *and* his erstwhile employers – who valued his inputs and, particularly, his enthusiastic and pragmatic knowledge of the design process. They also liked his 'out in the marketplace' sharpness and 'can-do' attitude. John was soon able to sell his production skills to other companies as well. When last heard of, he was setting up a small publishing company producing works for children with learning difficulties.

Although this is an ideal example of dovetailing it does make the point: it is possible to transfer from one rather limiting situation to another much more varied one without upsetting anyone, particularly oneself.

WHAT OTHERS MAY THINK

At this point in your process of checking out Portfolio Working it might be useful to share your thoughts and feelings with family. (I would suggest that for 'family' read immediate family, not in-laws, uncles, cousins or aunts – or those you only meet at weddings and funerals. You want to be dealing with people that know you pretty well.) There are two reasons for doing this.

First, they will probably have fears about the general drift of your interest and how it will affect them: fears that will need to be discussed openly and which may provide useful insights for you, into you, how you operate and what's realistic and what's not. Not that you have to agree with anything or everything family and friends say. Bear in mind also that irrational fear can easily be disguised as a rational argument. Freaking out is only one of many ways of saying: 'Oh, no you don't. Over my dead body!' or 'I'm really scared.'

Second, however, after the initial shock, they will almost certainly also have useful advice, suggestions for actions and even encouragement. None of us like to watch our loved ones going through a daily hell, especially if they're doing it partly to support us. So in most circumstances you could expect a reasonably positive response to the first timid flapping of your freedom wings.

One way to maximise helpful input from family and to minimise adverse reaction, while still allowing real fears to surface, is to adopt the dovetail principle again. By *gradually* introducing the possibility of your doing something else instead (or 'as well as') you give others the opportunity to participate in and therefore 'own' a part of the process – initially of exploration, later of decision – one way or the other. If they are involved from the very first stirrings, the process will seem a lot less threatening and you stand a chance of getting positive and reasonably objective input. Also, whatever you decide after the process, the decision and its consequences are shared more evenly.

So, don't necessarily keep it to yourself – but *do* choose the right moment.

Friends and some colleagues are also worth inviting into the process. But it will be a different process; their experience of you is clearly not the same as that of your family and, since there are less likely to be emotional complications, you may get a more objective reaction to what you are contemplating doing.

You will certainly get two major camps developing as you share your thoughts. The:

- 'You must be completely crazy to even think of changing things now. Just think, in a few years time, you could be Manager of Y Division and drive a BMW 7.1. Why throw all that away. Don't be a fool!' camp; and the
- 'God, you're really very brave. It sounds marvellous. I really admire you for going with your principles. I wish I had the courage to do something like that!' camp.

Again, as with family, the earlier you moot the idea with friends, the less likely you are to get extremely polarised reactions. Make them part of the process. And remember, the thing people like doing most of all (after talking about themselves) is to give advice. So let them share and help you build your visions. It's free, you may benefit and they'll have a wonderful time fantasising. (You never know, they may end up joining you.)

IT'S DOWN TO YOU

In the end though, it's your choice as to what you do and how you do it. That may sound obvious but look at it another way: we are all well trained in the art of avoidance and seeing to it that other people or outside circumstances 'make' our decisions for us. For example: 'I can't do *that* because s/he will be angry/hurt/sad.' By being open about your thoughts for the future, you can at least avoid avoidance and *own* your decisions.

Although it's not nearly time to make a decision about anything, at this point it would be useful to log any reactions you get from friends and family. And not just to log them. Try to put yourself in the place of the person who has just so vehemently thrown out your ideas for change. What is it in your proposals that is threatening them? Are their fears justified? How, by doing things differently, could you threaten them less? Or not at all? And, on the other hand, when someone stands there with that visionary far-away glow in their eyes, how much of that fulsome praise for your courage is a reflection of their own longings? Does that kind of reaction really serve you?

Also important is to log your reactions to the feedback you get. Try as far as possible to capture your *feelings* when you receive it, as well as your thoughts. Why, for example, did your heart sink to your boots when your mother drew herself up to her full height and said with an air of dignified resignation: 'I'm sure you're right, dear – you probably know best'? Is there just the slightest possibility of a well-entrenched behavioural control pattern here? Or when a friend who you admired tremendously and who you thought would be delighted for you and very supportive instead turned out to be less than enthusiastic – in fact, downright negative. Is it possible that your relationship up to now has had a strong element of you being Mr or Ms Sensible to their Mr or Ms Bright 'n Breezy? If that's true, they may be feeling threatened by your bid for better things, for a higher profile. Record your surprise. You need to 'listen' to those feelings, they are a very accurate barometer of what's going on for you.

We'll be talking more about feelings later. They are a far greater part of business life than many would care to admit.

PRE-FLIGHT CHECK

All the things I've asked you to do so far in this chapter are designed to give you a clearer idea of: where you are in your life, where you might want to be instead and what possibilities exist for getting there.

Again I want to stress that, as I said at the beginning, you may not wish to change to a Portfolio way of working. Be warned – it's not for everyone. Not everyone wants, or has to be, a test pilot.

At the very least, though, I hope you will have become a little clearer about yourself and, if your decision is *not* to entertain change, it will have been based on a few more considerations than were previously available.

Having said that, I hope your curiosity will take you on through the book as there are many useful ideas that you can usefully apply to a single, full-time job as well. Remember those Personal Development Plans (PDPs) I spoke of in the Introduction? This and the ensuing chapters contain essential material to help you develop

your PDP. Also, for those working with, or managing projects with, a Portfolio Person as part of the team, they are essential reading.
For those still on board . . . A final check . . .

THE PORTFOLIO AIRWAYS PRE-FLIGHT CHECK-LIST

Please tick those statements which apply to you. If some of them don't, that's fine, just add your own. If you're not happy writing in this book, photocopy these next few pages instead.

Part One – Where you want to be in your life in *five years' time* in terms of:

Family and Home

☐ I will be living in the same area as I am now
☐ I will be living in a better, safer and more desirable area
☐ I will be living somewhere simpler and quieter
☐ I will be living in a town or city
☐ I will be living in a rural area
☐ I will be living in .... (a different country)
☐ ....
☐ ....

☐ I will be living in the same house as I am now
☐ I will be living in the same flat as I am now
☐ I will be living in a bigger house
☐ I will be living in a bigger flat
☐ I will be living in a smaller house
☐ I will be living in a smaller flat
☐ ....
☐ ....

☐ I will be enjoying the garden I have now
☐ I will have a garden
☐ I will have a bigger garden
☐ I will have a swimming pool
☐ I will have a smaller and more manageable garden
☐ I will/will not have garden gnomes
☐ I will grow my own vegetables and fruit

- ☐ ....
- ☐ ....

- ☐ I will have the same neighbours as I have now
- ☐ I will have very friendly, socially active neighbours, always throwing parties
- ☐ I will have very friendly but quiet and undemanding neighbours
- ☐ I won't have any immediate neighbours at all
- ☐ ....
- ☐ ....

- ☐ I will have a child/children
- ☐ I will have another child/more children
- ☐ My child/ren will be at kindergarten
- ☐ My child/ren will be at good school/s and doing well
- ☐ My child/ren will be at university
- ☐ My child/ren will be happy surf bums on Bondi Beach
- ☐ My child/ren will have left home and become (relatively) independent
- ☐ I won't have children
- ☐ ....
- ☐ ....
- ☐ ....

- ☐ I will have the pets I have now
- ☐ I will have pets
- ☐ I will have more pets
- ☐ I won't have any pets
- ☐ ....
- ☐ ....

- ☐ The atmosphere in my home will be busy and active with lots of people coming and going all the time
- ☐ The atmosphere in my home will be peaceful and restful
- ☐ There will be a quiet place for me, my haven
- ☐ I will be living in a lighthouse
- ☐ ....
- ☐ ....

Love, Romance and Social Life

☐ I will have lots of wonderful, holiday romances
☐ I will have lots of uncomplicated relationships
☐ I will be in an uncommitted, fun relationship
☐ I will not be in a relationship
☐ I will be in a long-term relationship but without any ties or expectations
☐ I will be in a long-term, committed, ongoing relationship
☐ I will be with someone I want to marry and who wants to marry me
☐ I will be with someone who will love and care for me
☐ I will be with someone who I can love and care for
☐ I will be with my present partner
☐ I will be married to my present partner
☐ I will be separated or divorced
☐ ....
☐ ....

☐ I will have lots of fun friends who never get too heavy or serious
☐ I will have some close and deep friendships
☐ I will have lots more friends
☐ I will have just a few friends who I really want to be with
☐ I will be the life and soul of lots of parties
☐ I will enjoy cooking and entertaining lots of friends
☐ I will enjoy a peaceful time mostly with my partner
☐ I will be an active member of a sports or social club or amateur dramatics society
☐ ....
☐ ....

Training, Leisure, Sport and Hobbies

☐ I will have gained a/another degree/diploma from full time study
☐ I will have gained a/another degree/diploma from evening/part-time study
☐ I will be able to go to restaurants whenever I like
☐ I will be able to go to restaurants more often
☐ I will be able to go to better restaurants

☐ I will be able to go to the movies, theatre or opera when I wish
☐ I will have the freedom and the time to go to pubs and clubs on a regular basis

69

☐ I will be able to watch TV when I like – and watch what I like!

☐ I will have time to pursue my hobbies in order to:
  ☐ escape from life's pressures when I need to
  ☐ use more of my skills
  ☐ gain more knowledge about things and people
  ☐ supplement my income
  ☐ ....
  ☐ ....
☐ I will have found a/a new and highly satisfying hobby

☐ I will have improved my performance in my chosen sport/s
☐ I will have a chosen sport
☐ I will have time to enjoy sports in order to:
  ☐ keep fit
  ☐ look good and feel good
  ☐ let off steam and deal with the pressure
  ☐ meet other like-minded people
  ☐ meet a wonderful, athletic man/woman
  ☐ travel to interesting sporting events
  ☐ improve my social standing
  ☐ improve my golf handicap
  ☐ ....
  ☐ ....

☐ I will have time to travel and explore the world
☐ ....
☐ ....

Happiness, Contentment and Image

☐ I will have time for myself
☐ I will be able to enjoy solitude
☐ I will not be under pressure from others
☐ I will not be under pressure from myself

☐ I will have a wonderful
  ☐ car
  ☐ boat
  ☐ huge TV
  ☐ model railway

☐ hi-fi system
☐ ....
☐ ....
☐ ....
☐ ....
☐ ....

☐ My life will be filled with excitement and stimulation
☐ My life will be tranquil

☐ I will be a member of local charities and other worthy causes
☐ I will be a member of local/national pressure groups for beneficial change
☐ I will be a member of a political party and be active in that
☐ ....
☐ ....

☐ I will be a respected member of my community
☐ I will be asked to advise and be on steering committees
☐ ....
☐ ....

Work

☐ I will be at the top of my tree
☐ I will be on the board of directors
☐ I will have lots of perks and bonuses
☐ I will be recognised as the best in my field/department/company
☐ I will head a large team
☐ I will be influential in shaping the future of my company
☐ I will be running my own department
☐ I will be in charge of a whole division
☐ I will be highly valued
☐ ....
☐ ....

☐ I will be running my own small company
☐ I will be doing what I want to do
☐ I will not be doing things I don't want to
☐ I will not be doing things I don't believe in
☐ I will be in full control – my own boss

71

☐ I will be building up my own business
☐ ....
☐ ....

☐ I will want to go into the office/studio/workshop
☐ I will want to go home at 5pm
☐ I will be able to go home at 5pm
☐ I will enjoy staying late if I want to
☐ I will have time to do the administrative and maintenance jobs
☐ I will be working only
   ☐ 4 days a week
   ☐ 3 days a week
   ☐ 2 days a week
   ☐ ....
   ☐ ....
   ☐ ....

Part Two: Will your current working situation, your chosen work path, deliver the things you've selected above?

Money

☐ My current job/workstyle will pay for all the things I've selected
☐ My current job/workstyle will pay for some of the things I've selected
☐ My current job/workstyle will pay for a few of the things I've selected
☐ My current job/workstyle will just cover the basics
☐ I will have to augment my current job/workstyle in order to achieve what I want
☐ ....
☐ ....
☐ ....

Time

☐ My current job/workstyle will allow me a lot of time for myself, my family and friends
☐ My current job/workstyle will allow me some time for myself, my family and friends

☐ My current job/workstyle will allow me a little time for myself, my family and friends
☐ My current job/workstyle won't allow me time for myself, my family and friends
☐ My current job/workstyle will mean working most evenings and weekends
☐ ....
☐ ....
☐ ....

☐ My current job/workstyle will only be for a year
☐ My current job/workstyle will last for a few years
☐ I can see myself working in this job/workstyle for years to come
☐ ....
☐ ....
☐ ....

Contentment

☐ My current job/workstyle will bring me enormous contentment
☐ My current job/workstyle will bring me contentment regularly
☐ My current job/workstyle will bring me contentment occasionally
☐ My current job/workstyle is unlikely to bring me contentment right away
☐ ....
☐ ....
☐ ....

Part Three: What will be the costs/disadvantages in terms of family etc of pursuing your current job/workstyle?

Family and Home

☐ ....
☐ ....
☐ ....
☐ ....
☐ ....

Romance, Love, Social Life

- ☐ ....
- ☐ ....
- ☐ ....
- ☐ ....
- ☐ ....

Training, Leisure, Sport and Hobbies

- ☐ ....
- ☐ ....
- ☐ ....
- ☐ ....
- ☐ ....

Happiness, Contentment and Image

- ☐ ....
- ☐ ....
- ☐ ....
- ☐ ....
- ☐ ....

Part Four: If your current job/workstyle is unlikely to bring any or all of the things and qualities you ticked or listed in Part One, what do you need to add to your working pattern in order to achieve them?

For the material things

- ☐ ....
- ☐ ....
- ☐ ....
- ☐ ....
- ☐ ....
- ☐ ....
- ☐ ....

For the intangibles and qualities

- ☐ ....
- ☐ ....

☐ ....
☐ ....
☐ ....
☐ ....
☐ ....

How does it feel to have completed this check-list? Has it been a case of confirmation that you're on track, heading in the right direction? Or has it brought a lot of unresolved issues to the surface? Either is great.

You may have had enough check-lists by now to last you until next Christmas, never mind the end of this book. The bad news is that are more to come – the good news is, not many are in the next chapter. Instead, we'll be looking at what you need to know to get started on a Portfolio Career.

Chapter summary

- There is no time for boredom in a Portfolio Career – it is filled with novelty and variety.
- With a Portfolio Career, you can choose what you do and who you do it with.
- Insights, skills and experience can be cross-networked to all tasks.
- Time management is crucial.
- Portfolio Careers are more than simply a way of earning a living.
- Portfolio Working will *not* be for everyone.
- The seven-hour itch – when do you get yours?
- Where are you in relation to your work – satisfied, delighted, bored, angry, fearful?
- How is your vision – where, what and who are you aiming to be?
- How abundant is your life right now?
- How gifted are you?
- Carrying out your personal SWOT analysis.
- Learning to love your hateful job and seeing it as the springboard into the next phase of your life.
- Successfully dovetailing your present with your future.
- Checking what others may think – family and friends – and honestly assessing their feedback.
- Avoiding avoidance and making your own decisions.
- The Portfolio Airways Pre-Flight Check-list.

Chapter Five

Getting started – what you need to know

The tangibles and intangibles you'll need to prepare you for your Portfolio Career – and for working alongside Portfolio People.

'Don't Should on Yourself'
Sign on Barry and Gloria Blum's kitchen door, Mill Valley, California.

> *'This happens fairly regularly:*
> *I'm dancing about with excitement at my latest break in one of my portfolio of activities. My companion sighs with relief and says: "Well, now you can give up the other job at last."*
> *or . . .*
> *"Oh, I see, so this is your hobby then."*

Kate Codrington, Portfolio Person.

The first thing to say is that you don't *really* need this book to get you started on a Portfolio Career – it's mostly common sense. However . . .

One or two things may help. Such as how to deal with the emotional 'ups' and 'downs' you'll experience if you decide to go Portfolio. Forgiving yourself, for example. Or Motivation Maintenance. Then there's learning to live in the Now, handling Uncertainty and riding Change. Followed by learning Trust, dealing with Doubt and growing your intuition. You'll certainly need a dash of Courage, a pinch of Cheek and bags of Curiosity – and you thought this was a book about work?

It is.

The mechanics of business are the easy bit. It's the emotions that bite. And those you'll experience as a Portfolio Person are no different from the ones you get in full-time employment – except that there will be more of them and they will also be stronger.

Because a lot of the time you'll be on your own with no one to share them with, even if it's simply chatting round the coffee machine and letting the others in your department know that you're under pressure that week, that the 'old man' is on your back or 'Sales are screaming for their figures'. You will have to learn how to deal with the highs and lows on your own most of the time.

This chapter won't give you all the answers but it will warn you of the questions lying in wait and offer some suggestions.

Later, we *do* get to be 'practical'. We touch on how to deal with bureaucracy (no accounts department between you and the taxman now), and how best to equip yourself, both with people and things. Finally, we take an overview of essential disciplines and routines.

First, let's look at some typical hopes and fears around the idea of becoming a Portfolio Person, taken from the questionnaires I always hand out at workshops and talks.

Hopes:
'That I will wake up in the morning and feel that it is great to be alive.'
'That I'll be living life more fully.'
'That I will get to meet interesting people.'
'That I'll never be bored.'
'That I'll have a flexible time frame.'
'That I'll become rich and famous.'
'That I will be free from ties to only one area of work.'
'That I will make more money.'
'That I'll be less stressed.'
'That I will be able to get the most out of the many skills I have.'
'That I'll survive!'

Fears:
'That I won't have a regular income.'
'That I'll burn out.'
'That I won't be able to cope with the money side/pensions/tax etc.'
'That I'd lack focus.'
''That I won't be able to find the work.'
'That I'll be scattered.'
'That no one will value and want what I have to offer.'
'That I won't be able to balance the different jobs and that they'll conflict.'

'That I'll experience insecurity, lack of money and over commit-ment.'
'That there won't be someone to tell me what to do next.'
'That I won't find the energy.'

Which of those do you identify with? Make a note in your pad.

You'd think that with some of the hopes expressed here there would be nothing stopping them. Yet we are often held back by something, prevented from reaching our visions, rooted firmly to the spot, however uncomfortable or unfulfilling.

SHOULDING

I'd like to introduce a new word here, the verb: 'to should'. Most of us are really good at it. Another way of putting it is 'to beat yourself up over something you think you have to do or be'. Recognise it? There you are, grinding your teeth over some task or other that you absolutely know you don't want to be doing, hating it so much that you become paralysed with anger and resentment and can't do it properly anyway. And why? Because you think you have to do it. That it's expected of you. By whom? Probably, if you looked into it, no one – except yourself.

Some people have spent their entire lives doing something they loathed because they thought their fathers expected it or would think less of them if they didn't. Actually, their fathers probably couldn't care less, providing their offspring were happy, but the sons and daughters forgot to check.

So check. Who is really expecting you to do what you do? Have you asked them if this is the case? Recently?

There are, of course, some things you *will* have to do which are difficult or boring. But, however awful they may seem, there is usually some sense or purpose in them. In these cases, focus on the finiteness of the task. Break the time up into mini-targets and turn it into a game. (The Power of Pottering, in Chapter 8, will help too.)

In either case, taking your energy out of fighting the situation will help. I remember some years ago when I was into yoga, wearing flimsy boxers and a tee-shirt in a very cold church hall, holding dhanurasana posture and feeling frozen and miserable. I suddenly had the notion to explore the feeling of cold, to go into it and experience it rather than fight it. The extraordinary thing was, once I did this, I didn't feel cold anymore. Having taken my energy and focus out of the fighting, the cold went.

BLOWING IT

In the first week of my first job as a very junior architectural assistant I was allowed, between fetching lunch-time sandwiches and brewing tea, to make a few simple alterations to a large and valuable ink drawing. Full of enthusiasm, I perched a bottle of black ink on the top of the drawing board where, inevitably, it tipped over and ink ran all down the drawing. In an effort to rescue the situation, I tipped the board up and the ink ran all the way back again, completing an attractive crisscross pattern of little rivulets. I shall always admire and appreciate the generosity of the architect in charge for not firing me – or despising me either.

You see, making mistakes is a very important activity. They say the old ones are the best ones and one of the most ancient truisms tells us that 'we learn by our mistakes'. I certainly did back then.

Right now we seem increasingly to be in a society that doesn't allow us to make mistakes, that apparently doesn't want us – or it – to learn. In our quantity-orientated places of work it's extremely unusual to expect a positive response from your colleagues if you've goofed over something. You're more likely to get a black mark against your name in the invisible pecking order and concerned glances from your colleagues implying sympathy over a possible change in your circumstances. It follows that we sometimes put a huge effort into concealing our screw-ups and then into worrying that someone will find out. In this way we carry our mistakes around with us like millstones, not as part of our rich experience.

The more we can see life as an exploration – as something profoundly fascinating to be looked into, when everything we do takes on the nature of an experiment – then mistakes can become a valuable part of the process. We can take the negativity out of them.

This is not to invite irresponsibility or the abandonment of vigilance and foresight. It is to encourage the notion that there is something to be learned from any situation, if we are open to it. Nor do I advocate making the same 'mistakes' over again. There's no learning in blind repetition.

Remember also: forgive yourself. Other people may forgive you, but *you* will need to as well – and that can be very hard, especially if you are on your own.

Put the past behind you, as useful experience: not in front, as a reproach, always in your way to trip you up.

RIDING THE EMOTIONAL ROLLER-COASTER

As I discovered in the freezing yoga class, we can manage extremes of feeling by allowing rather than fighting them. At times you will feel absolutely terrified, and will need to go into the feeling, not with your intellect – that will probably tell you that this is a load of mumbo jumbo anyway – but with your feelings. Locate where the terror is – perhaps in your solar plexus, perhaps in your mouth and throat – and check how it feels, acknowledge it as a temporary reality and give it time. Don't rush it. It will diminish and eventually go.

Sometimes you will feel rage, so rage – but ideally, you'll vent the emotions on cushions rather than people. Don't bottle it up. Try to express it in a safe environment even if that means shouting at the sky on a deserted hillside at midnight. Better still do something physical like digging the allotment or going for a brisk walk. I once knew a housewife who spent most of the day on her own, trapped in a comfortably dull home and surrounded by the shiny appliances her regularly absent husband had given her as a substitute for his love. She hated her situation, her house and her family but, since she also loved them and believed there wasn't a way of expressing her pain without hurting them, she cleaned instead. She gave the floors, the walls, the furnishings, the clothes, everything, absolute hell. Every day. The family put the immaculate condition of the home down to motherly love.

Be prepared for mood swings. You will experience moments of euphoria, of great satisfaction, of massive doubt, of great fear. Remember that fear is frozen excitement. Euphoria is freed excitement. The excitement is the same, it's what we do with it that makes the difference.

Dealing effectively with your fear is probably the most important business skill you will need to develop. At one extreme it can be terror which, if allowed free rein, will cloud your judgement, shrivel your courage and distort your decisions. At the other, it can be your vigilance, protecting you from making unwise investments or stepping onto the street without checking for buses first. You need to be in the place in between.

The two worst kinds of fear in my experience are of sudden, frightening events, where one is shocked into disempowerment, and the more pervading fear of not knowing what is going to happen – a fear of the future. The first kind is hard to guard against, except by learning to rely on one's innate common sense and instinct of self-preservation. In the second case, planning for specific eventualities can be reassuring, since in most cases one can assess the consequences of a course of action and, if necessary, prepare for the worst case scenario.

MY MOST FEAR-FULL MOMENTS LIST

Please note in your pad some the most fearful experiences in your life, differentiating between sudden shocks and 'not knowing' situations. Then mark with a tick those that would not have been nearly so bad if you'd done a bit of research into likely consequences rather than hiding, quaking under the proverbial duvet.

MOTIVATION MAINTENANCE

Usually we are motivated by excitement, in its fear form or its euphoria form. We can also be motivated by staying on the comforting rails of a familiar routine. A lot of people are motivated by fear of loss. Of what they will lose if they 'don't'. Of what will happen if they 'do'. It could manifest as not applying for your boss's job when it comes vacant, in case you don't get it or not asking someone out, in case you get rejected.

Occasionally we spring out of bed in a moment of pure *joie de vivre*. But not usually because we're dying to get to the office. More likely something to do with leaving for an exotic holiday or because it's a particularly wonderful sunny day with the prospect of a leisurely breakfast on the terrace.

As a Portfolio Person you won't have a boss to 'help' you out of bed in the morning. You'll have to take on that role yourself. You will, however, have lots of opportunities for long breakfasts. Which is delightful – and dangerous. A realistic – and I mean realistic – routine is the answer. You *will* need to give yourself time to enjoy a good start to the day, otherwise you'll go through it resenting the fact that you didn't and spoil everything else.

Taking time for yourself is crucial – more of that in Chapter 8.

Rewards are another way of helping to maintain motivation. Treating yourself like a child who gets treats for being good may be one way. Sounds silly, doesn't it? But it can work. Try it now. Three mornings in the office by 8am this week = croissants for breakfast the fourth morning. Don't set your targets too high or you won't get any treats. Remember avoidance? Don't set your targets too low, either, or you'll get fat.

BEING FULLY IN THE NOW

Some famous wag said 'the British walk backwards into the future looking lovingly at the past'. In Europe we *are* a bit hung up on our history. Rather scared of novelty. But there are also many who inhabit the Wonderful World of When.

As with most things, we need balance. We can dream our past away: or our future. If we are always preoccupied with what has been, with how everything was somehow less complicated, safer, sunnier or more ordered, we'll be hard put to do what we need to do right now. If we are always fantasising about what we are going to do – one day, soon, when the circumstances are right – our focus will be so far ahead that we'll trip over what's right in front of us.

It sounds terribly obvious, but think of the success of the nostalgia industry. All those reproduction thatched cottage teapots, made in China rather than of it. And the increasingly electronic Fantasy Future Industry – virtually virtual anything. We *are* increasingly insulated from immediate reality. It's more comfortable that way: but how can we be effective and fulfilled if there's a great hole in the middle of our awareness? And how can we be effective and fulfilled if, when we are in the Now, we resent it and long to escape, backwards or forwards?

PP Tip: put everything you have into whatever you are doing, however trivial. Do the washing up beautifully. You'll be surprised at the results!

82

HANDLING UNCERTAINTY

One of the things we can be certain of is uncertainty. It has always been with us and always will be. It is one of the most crippling forms of fear. In a state of uncertainty we fear loss: loss of life at its most extreme; loss of love; loss of face; loss of possessions; loss of control.

So, in a state of uncertainty, let's look now at what it is you might lose. Be quite specific. List everything.

Now list all the things you *can't* lose. If you need a reminder, go back to your Wealth List in the previous chapter.

As we've already noted, the fear of not knowing about something is usually far greater than the fear of knowing about it, however dire that something may be. Therefore, you'll want to find out what you can about the circumstances surrounding what you experience as uncertainty.

Remember too that uncertainty can be a timely reminder to check over your inventory of assets, to see whether they need some attention.

A feeling of uncertainty can also be a useful reminder that change may be around the corner. Check it out. Now.

List all the things that might change in your life – and don't forget the good things.

It's a lot, isn't it?

COPING WITH CHANGE

As with uncertainty, there will always be change. Our bodies are doing it whether we like it or not. Other people are changing things around us whether we like it or not. Even under that duvet, we can't escape change. Sometimes we like change, sometimes we don't, depending on whether we feel we have some control over it or not. As for 'imposed' change, we can either view it as a bulldozer or a bus. One we will try to avoid: one we may climb aboard, once we've checked the destination. Or we could hide in the ditch. It's up to us. The more bus rides we take, though, the more countryside we'll get to see.

Generally, it's the effects of any change that we fear rather than the actual change itself. So, if we can take our focus out of fearing the consequences and look instead at where change might really lead us, we might feel a lot better about it. As with uncertainty, we need the facts, not the fiction. It also helps to stop using the word 'change' and to substitute the word 'transformation' which is much more exciting – and less scary.

The pace of evolution *is* pretty scary. A look at *The Gaia Atlas of Planet Management* and the pages which depict the growth of population and mobility and the development of information transfer and energy use, for example, will show a curve starting very gently in the plains of hunter-gatherer man, climbing up to the foothills of medieval man and rising alarmingly through the Industrial Revolution and the 20th Century to the vertical face of today.* Up here, the air is rarer, the weather a lot more unpredictable and there will be avalanches. You bet.

TUNING IN TO TRUSTING

Trust is the opposite of fear. If you can practise dealing with your fear as I've indicated above you can clear the way for Trust. I know that the more I trust, the more I *can* trust. More importantly, the more I can trust, the more that trust is justified. I am not talking about blind trust, that doesn't serve anyone since it excludes intuition – see below.

Of course, we have to balance our trust with vigilance. It's more a case of gradual experimentation, almost as if there's a particular wavelength we can tune into where things really work. If I'm on that wavelength, I find that buses arrive perfectly on time, I meet exactly the right person or I walk onto a platform with two minutes to spare and still get a seat on the train. It's something to do with trusting that what is happening right now is fine. Funny thing, though, once doubt starts to creep in, I blow it and the day begins to go wrong.

I remember on one occasion I really had to catch a particular train but needed to get a newspaper, buy stamps and post a letter first – as well as buy a ticket. There were very few minutes left when I arrived at the station. I relaxed, bought the paper and the stamps, posted the letter and stood in line for the ticket. Despite the length of time the person up front was taking, I stayed calm and trusting that everything would be OK. I released any anxiety I had about the consequences of not being on that train. The time for the train came

* *The Gaia Atlas of Planet Management*, published 1985 by Pan Books.

and went – so did the train. I eventually got my ticket and asked about the next train. A much faster one was leaving in six minutes, giving me enough time to get a coffee.

I should warn you: it doesn't always work this way. Nevertheless, increasingly, I find I can *choose* not to be hassled and that somehow, in this frame of mind, events seem to flow seamlessly one after the other. It can feel like staying on top of everything all day long or, as the surfers say in Hawaii, *he'enalu*, sliding on a wave.

So, try it for yourself, gently at first. Don't start deliberately missing trains, but do experiment. Pick a time when it's not 'life and death'. Observe yourself in the situation – how did you do? Did you manage to tune into that calm, hassle-free wavelength – and stay on it?

> **PP Tip:** Do start the day as you mean to go on. If you hop about on one foot doing your earrings with one hand and waving your breakfast toast around with the other, you'll probably spend the whole day hopping.

When it comes to trusting others, remember that they will also need to be able to trust you (more of this in Chapter 10).

> **PP Tip:** Focus wholly on the service you're giving to a client, their need, their aspirations, not what they're going to pay you; then trust that if you get that bit right, the money will follow, because it will.

DEALING WITH DOUBT

Generally, doubt is an absence of trust but it can also, in the form of self-doubt, be fear of success. Sometimes failure – or a state of not being successful – is easier to handle than success. Success is scary. That same parapet that provides protection from would-be snipers, when something nasty is going on, can also shade you from the dazzling sunshine of success. Most of us spend quite a lot of time sitting well below the parapet for one reason or another.

Success can mean a lot of hard work (usually in a hurry) and a lot more responsibility. This can be disquieting if you like a peaceful existence. Suddenly there seem to be a lot more people in the world and you've acquired a huge number of friends you never knew you had. Who can blame you for keeping your head down?

An ambivalent attitude towards success may come across as a lack of confidence. This will transmit itself to potential clients via your voice and your body language, so you'll need to spend time working on your belief in yourself and your abilities. It can be helpful to collate all those glowing testimonials and letters of thanks into a handy folder, or start a 'Compliments Book'. This is a little book in which you write all the nice, complimentary, praising, honouring and downright flattering things people say about you. You don't have to show it to anyone if you're embarrassed – but you should really pin the best ones up on the wall where you can see them every time you're at your workstation.

Doubts about other people are often reflections of how we feel about some aspects of ourselves. What is it that we doubt in that person? If it's their lack of punctuality, is this highlighting our own fears around being late? Many of your reservations may be unfounded. Those that prove to have been justified need to be aired if possible. I'll cover this in Chapter 11, Relationships.

GROWING YOUR INTUITION

Intuition is experienced in a number of different ways. It can be a flash of insight. It can be a little voice somewhere in your head saying something apparently unconnected with anything else. It can be a deep conviction that something is so, an incontrovertible truth. Often, these manifestations of intuition cannot be easily put into words. This is because once we start to mix intuition with language, thus passing it through an intellectual filter, it can be distorted, even destroyed. So it is important not to try to explain it – to others or yourself. It is best just to accept.

Quite often in my work, I listen to my 'inner voice', as I call my intuition. Sometimes it comes up with some really 'off-the-wall' insights but they nearly always turn out to be spot on in the context I'm working in. I've given up questioning it because I know that as soon as any doubt comes into my mind, the insight disappears. So now I trust it.

Intuition is, therefore, an extremely powerful tool – and a very delicate one.

Intuition is also close to feeling. It is important here to point out that feelings and emotions are very different. Feelings are a very fine diagnostic instrument if we 'listen' to them. They can tell us what's going on inside us. Emotions, on the other hand, are unreliable since they are generally our reactions to what's going on outside – up one minute, down the next. Emotions are the habitat of fear and anger. Feelings are the source of our truth.

COURAGE, CHEEK AND CURIOSITY

You'll need all three in generous quantities. The good news is, like muscle-tone, they develop with use.

Courage is essential if you are ever to move out of familiar territory, to gird up your entrepreneurial loins and treat the world not as a shark-infested sea but as an oyster bed with pearls to be plucked. You'll want to think of yourself as a Livingston – but don't necessarily expect a Stanley.

Once you've taken the plunge, you'll need a degree of cheek to get you through the obstacles (secretaries, deputies and good old-fashioned scepticism) to the point where people you might do business with are interested in you. Most people admire friendly persistence and are a little envious of good-humoured cheek. They are not impressed by timidity. Cheek can take you far.

Once you've got face to face with the possible prospect, you are going to have to remember that he or she who asks the questions controls the conversation. Asking questions first gives you a chance to gauge the sort of person you are dealing with and what their needs are. This will also be a perfect opportunity to use your intuition. In order to maintain a series of intelligent questions that attract answers, you'll need to really *want* to know how the company operates, how long it's been going, when your contact joined, what really interests them (the 'hot spot' in sales-speak), where the problems lie that you may be able to help solve and so on.

This is where your curiosity will come into play. Together with your ability to listen and your enthusiasm. If you are simply asking questions as a means to an end, like a routine pre-flight check, they will quickly pick this up, because a mechanical attitude is likely to produce a mechanical tone of voice. If you are genuinely interested in how their company produces rubber grommets, they will begin to make a friend of you. People love talking about themselves and most people like dealing with people they like.

Not interested in rubber grommets? Why not? Wouldn't you like someone to be really interested in and enthusiastic about what *you* do?

PP Tip: Only wimps pretend they know; real courage is not being afraid to ask.

Curiosity will also guide you through unfamiliar territory. It usually feels safer to pass by a possible opportunity than to stop and look into it. Your curiosity will need to be capable of overcoming your reticence. I don't mean you should go barging in, rather that your natural interest should be allowed to make connections for you. You'll need to let it and you'll need to learn a lot of new information, so you'd better be prepared. A large notebook will help.

Abraham Maslow recommended that we expose ourselves to new experiences and activities even when we're unsure which direction our life is taking. He describes a 'self-actualiser' – someone who is contented, regardless of problems, creative and spontaneous, fun and unbound by convention. To become one may mean: not always sticking with the safe routines, questioning views held by others – particularly those in authority – being familiar with your own feelings, expressing your own views honestly and taking responsibility for them and having a positive attitude toward everything you do and toward others.

GOLDEN OPPORTUNITIES AND RED HERRINGS

As a courageous, cheeky and curious Portfolio Person, getting out and about and seeing lots of people, you will come regularly into contact with possible projects and freelance job opportunities. Since your most precious asset is your time, you'll need to be able to choose wisely where to invest it. Deciding which on your list of 'hot prospects' are genuinely worth putting effort into and which are a waste of space will be very important.

It is not easy, there are no set rules. The most reliable way of choosing whether to go for something is to check your feelings about it and the people already involved in it, and then let your intuition work on both. A lot of us do this already without realising it – going on a hunch, we call it, or gut instinct. But the important thing to remember is that the less emotion there is around the decision, the better the intuitive insight is likely to be. Your feelings will give you the best chance of an honest appraisal of whether you could carry out the task. Your emotions may bring out your fear as neediness, make you too eager and cloud your judgement.

As an architect, I was regularly besieged by building materials salesmen. I didn't much like the 'over-pally', pushy and overtly 'hungry' ones. So, although they may not have known it, they had a much tougher job to persuade me. The ones I appreciated most were those who saw their role as using their experience to quietly help with identifying my needs, with no apparent expectation of an immediate sale. They earned my loyalty and, if it was appropriate, I would always specify their products.

Clearly, the more information you can glean, the better. To be well-informed is to be well-equipped.

However, there's no point in going after something you know very little about – which is where networking comes in. Being able to recommend 'someone who can' is useful as it keeps you in contact with your client, important if you're going to develop a good long-term relationship with them. They will almost certainly expect you to stay in touch.

Having said that, there *is* the 'can do' factor. The US and Asia is full of it. We could do with a bit more in the UK. If there's not very much else around, what's to stop you doing something new? If you can fix clocks why not do it for a little money? Or as a favour? The task doesn't have to be wrapped up in bright paper with 'Job' stamped all over it. One of the benefits of portfolio working is that you can take on the odd 'not-in-the-job-description' type job occasionally. It's great for self-esteem and you certainly won't be bored.

Some of the most important parts of my Portfolio are there because I applied the 'can do' factor as opposed to the 'don't know' or 'not sure' factor. I would not, of course, have accepted an invitation to perform brain surgery, but all my business counselling stems from the attitude: 'If I can do something to help, fine; if there's something I can't do, I'll say so.' I have never pretended to be an expert, just someone that might be able to help. If the potential client liked the look of me, they gave me the job.

So be open to new ideas, situations and people. Give them your full attention before you decide to follow up or reject them.

I'll deal in detail with saying 'no' in Chapter 9.

PP Tip: If in doubt, stick to what you know and are comfortable doing. You don't get any thanks for screwing up, you get writs. Balance the temptation to say 'yes' to everything with the ability to say 'no' when you need to.

LEARNING TO LOVE THE TAX OFFICE

As a Portfolio Person you will have to deal with a few more layers of bureaucracy than you do in full-time employment. Up to now, for example, most of your tax affairs will have been in the hands of an accounts department and all you've had to do is spend what's left after the tax office have had their slice. Generally, they will make sure you pay enough but not too much tax and will build any special circumstances, allowances etc into the equation. If you are self-employed you have to take on these functions yourself, so you will come into much more direct contact with the tax office.

If I said that tax inspectors were not ogres but just humans like the rest of us, most of you would agree and accuse me of stating the obvious. (Some of you, however, might not!) Why is it then that we invest so much fear in our tax authorities? How many times have you put those official brown envelopes to the bottom of the pile of post? Or, perhaps, left them for a day or two to be dealt with 'later'? I have clients who have had deep drawers full of brown envelopes to be dealt with 'later', many of them years old. It's like having a worry bin instead of a waste bin. At least the waste gets emptied regularly.

It's not just that they usually mean money. I've found that the biggest fear is because for many people they represent a loss of control. Tax affairs are very complex and it's a lot to expect someone for whom tax calculations are an occasional, part-time activity to be fully conversant with all the subtleties and quirks in the system. After all, an entire industry has grown up around taxes and avoiding them.

There are basically two options: you can hand everything over to an accountant, in which case you will still need to insist on regular and thorough updates in order to remain in control. Or you can handle it yourself – the cheaper but more stressful option.

In either case you would be well advised to meet and set up a good working relationship with your tax-office representative. In my experience, they are nearly always extremely courteous, helpful and patient – also in dishing out advice – providing you treat them with respect and honesty. More of this in Chapter 11.

THE SOFTWARE YOU NEED TO RUN YOUR BUSINESS

By software I don't mean floppy disks – I mean people, and specifically, the team you gather about you.

I'll go into detail on this aspect of Portfolio Working in Chapter 11, but you will need to put serious time into establishing good relationships with everyone you come into contact with in your portfolio career. If you're currently working with a large company, you probably take most of your support for granted.

On your own, you will need to consider who to have in your team. Will you need an accountant? Or a solicitor? On a continuous, occasional or 'stand-by' basis? Will you be maintaining all your financial records yourself or should you use a bookkeeper? How about a person Friday? Are people who telephone you going to be happy with a robotic answerphone voice, or will they prefer the real thing?

Investigate your options, and talk to friends, ex-colleagues and other freelancers about the support systems they use – including what they really deliver and how much they cost. It will be time well spent.

Setting up a support team doesn't mean you'll be able to just sit back and watch the clockwork whirring. There'll be quite a lot of winding to be done to keep things ticking over. You'll find that getting someone else to do something for you will not free all the time you gain from not doing it yourself. If you're not careful, you could end up spending most of your time managing your support team and doing very little actual fee-earning work yourself. You'll need to learn how to manage your managing. Although there are many hundreds of Management 'how to' books, there are really no hard and fast rules to rely on – just guidelines that will suit some and not others. It's up to you – again! Through trial, and error (and more error) and over time, you'll find your way of doing things.

Even with a brilliant support team, you will still need to be in complete control and take full responsibility for decisions. Apart from helping you do the actual work, the administrative role of your team will be to provide you with pre-digested, summarised but accurate information on which to base those decisions. As time goes on, of course, relationships will develop to the point where some of this can be delegated, but don't forget that it's ultimately down to you to run a tight ship.

How much interface you have with the members of your team is up to you – but building in time to maintain those relationships is essential and you might consider setting aside regular times for each. In a situation where you have a group of part-time employees, for example, a regular weekly forum can be invaluable to discuss management and administrative activities and air important issues and concerns. I'm always surprised at how rarely such an obviously essential management process is implemented.

SELECTING THE RIGHT HARDWARE

What you need in the way of equipment depends very much on what you are going to be doing. This sounds terribly obvious, but you'd be surprised. Although there are some essentials, every office will be different so don't feel there's an archetype you have to conform to. Design it around your needs, not the glossies in the office equipment catalogue. The realities of your budget will probably help with this.

Before you buy – and all this gear is not cheap – consider and list all the jobs in your portfolio, the likely scenarios they will generate and the kind of equipment they will each demand. Also, since so much emphasis is now placed on 'instant' communication, list the different ways in which you expect to need to be in touch with people. Do you really need that Home page on the World Wide Web if, working as a gardener, most of your transactions take place on your clients' lawns?

What you will almost certainly need in addition to a telephone is a fax, an answerphone (or answering service) and a PC with enough memory. If you'll be travelling a great deal, a good laptop computer is worth considering. You can use it on trains and in hotel rooms. Internet connection may follow close behind so allow for this in any decisions about phone lines. These are the basic essentials.

Until next week, that is.

The problem is, by the time you read this, there may well be yet another clutch of electronic toys to tempt us. Ways of communicating and accessing information are proliferating wildly. Already there are personal organisers with a built-in phone and fax function, and the mobile office, sitting there on the car seat next to you, is a way of life for many salesmen. Video and tele-conferencing are becoming 'big-time'. So talk to colleagues, read the odd journal, drop in on your local office equipment outlet, keep informed and double check on what's just about to become available before you spend. You don't want to be left with outdated or over-priced hardware in a few months' time if you can avoid it.

If you are going to be one of the growing band of home workers, if at all possible dedicate a room in your home to your business, and keep children and dogs firmly out of it. You are probably going to need to hold occasional meetings, so consider whether you need access to a hired meeting venue on a regular basis (a professional environment adds a great deal to a presentation). It can be done 'on the cheap'. I regularly use five-star hotel lounges for business meetings and all it costs is a few mineral waters. (And the best places always have a constantly replenished bowl of those delicious Japanese seaweed snacks!). Try it before you sign up for some expensive venue. Or hire a hotel room for the day. A wily old colleague told me once that image consciousness is a killer for small businesses; too many expensive overheads. As far as he was concerned, the only good image was a healthy bottom line, and he did all his business in places that other people had to maintain.

A WORD ON THE MOBILE PHONE

If your portfolio of work is organised so that you never have to leave your office, and you do all your communicating by telephone, fax or internet, a mobile phone is not a great deal of use. If, on the other hand, you are always on the move and difficult to reach during the day a mobile phone is essential, particularly if it has a voice-mail facility.

I have to confess to having mixed feelings about mobile phones. Have you noticed how many people talk to themselves in public these days? And then you see the phone glued to their ear. There are phones in restaurants, phones on the train, on the buses even. Is it the fascinated embarrassment of listening to other people's conversation that makes us cringe, or the appalling banality of most overheard conversations?

If you do invest in a mobile phone, use the 'off' switch liberally. They do leave you wide open to interruption at the wrong moment, like in a meeting with another client or at a concert. Even at other moments they can be intrusive, for instance those important periods of integrative daydreaming in the car while the events of the day find their place in the filing cabinet of the mind.

David Nicholson-Lord has a further objection: '. . . mobile phones abolish time and place. They compress geography to vanishing point. If you are instantly available and accessible – if you are everywhere all the time – you are nowhere any of the time.'*

However, when you're sat in a traffic jam and late for a meeting, they are a godsend.

EVERYTHING BUT THE COFFEE MACHINE

There are a few things you need to have with you at all times, in and out of the office. I always carry with me:
- some of my three different lots of note paper and fax header sheets;
- a few blank invoices (you never know . . .);
- envelopes of assorted sizes;
- stamps, recorded delivery and special delivery forms (saves lots of time in the post office);
- my terms of reference and trading conditions. (If you don't have any, think very seriously about getting some; meanwhile a simple statement of the way you work is a good idea.);
- copies of testimonials and letters of thanks from clients;
- my career profile (short and pithy version, no histories);
- sample cashflows and time-planners;
- brochures/leaflets for the trusts I represent;
- timetables and train/bus route maps;
- *A to Z* of London;
- business cards (mine) and a business card album (for other people's);
- two different business network directories;
- post-it notes and note pad;
- adhesive tape, glue, paper clips and mini-stapler;
- coloured pens and markers;
- a small screwdriver (brilliant for tightening connections on the back of computers);
- back-up disks of important records and documents;

* David Nicholson-Lord writing in *Resurgence* magazine, No. 169.

- spare, formatted disks;
- a calculator;
- a corkscrew (this has proved *really* useful);
- a small, telescopic umbrella;
- finally, my Filofax, containing my diary and address-book.

This may seem somewhat over the top, and my briefcase is famously heavy, but I travel with the confidence of self-sufficiency, knowing that I can respond to most situations without the frustration of not having what I need to hand.

ESSENTIAL DISCIPLINES AND ROUTINES

The essentials are: time management, focus and commitment, trust and relationships. Add to these financial footwork and you have the guts of a Portfolio Career. These are all interdependent but I have sought to separate them as best I can to clarify the key issues around each. They are covered in detail in Chapters 8 through 12.

As I have said already, *the* most difficult part of running a portfolio career is Time Management. Chapter 8 deals with this in detail but the one thing I want to emphasise is the importance of taking time for yourself. I don't mean the odd snatched moment while you have a cup of coffee. Or the occasional hour while you're on a train and just gazing out at the scenery, although this is very important too, as we'll see later. Nor do I mean time with family, although that is also essential. I really do mean time for yourself. Time you can really call your own. Time that doesn't have to be filled with frenetic activity – unless you choose. Time that can be squandered without guilt.

In Chapter 9 we'll look at focus and the problem of staying concentrated on what is in front of you right now while at the same time keeping everything else going too. It's rather like being a Chinese Circus plate spinner with your eyes closed. Focus is also about not taking on too much, about concentrating your energy and, above all, about putting your commitment where it will serve you and your clients best.

We have already looked at trust and mentioned relationships. These are looked at in more detail in Chapters 10 and 11 respectively. Chapter 12, Financial Footwork, goes through the basics of financial control and record keeping based on lessons I have learned rather than expert advice from an accountant, so it is from (sometimes) bitter experience and not theory.

In the next chapter there will be more checklists on the assumption that what you've read so far hasn't put you off the idea completely.

Chapter Summary

- Your hopes for your Portfolio Career.
- Your fears around your Portfolio Career.
- 'Shoulding' on yourself – who's expecting you to do this?
- The importance of making mistakes.
- Riding the emotional roller-coaster and dealing with fear.
- Your worst moments list.
- Maintaining your motivation – what gets you out of bed?
- Being in the 'Now' – balancing between past and future and doing the washing up beautifully.
- Handling uncertainty – compiling your loss list.
- Coping with change – compiling your changes list and seeing it as something potentially positive.
- Tuning into the trust wavelength – surfing your day.
- Dealing with doubt – why are you behind the parapet?
- Growing your intuition and learning how to tell the difference between emotions and feelings.
- Travelling with courage, cheek and curiosity in your backpack and putting them to good use.
- Golden opportunities and red herrings – knowing how to tell the difference, the 'can do' factor and saying 'no'.
- Dealing successfully with bureaucracy – learning to love the tax office and getting them on your side.
- Assembling your team and how to get the most support from them.
- Equipping yourself with the right hardware – just enough techno toys for your needs.
- The mobile phone debate – where are you with them?
- What you need to have with you at all times.

Chapter Six

Getting started – check-lists and manuals

The essential documents and charts you'll need to produce and a Survival Check-list to help you prepare for the worst and the best.

> *All the world's a stage,*
> *And all the men and women merely players;*
> *They have their exits and their entrances,*
> *And one man in his time plays many parts*
>
> *Shakespeare, 'As You Like It'.*

The check-lists that follow are designed to help prepare you for actually being a Portfolio Person. The more thoroughly you follow them the more prepared you'll be and, moreover, the more you'll have thought about the issues that you will have to tackle. If it's easier, copy the check-lists out in your pad or scan them into your PC and work on them there.

We'll start with a Survival Check-list, as this is your bottom line, your fall-back position. We'll do a simple cashflow projection. Then we'll spend some time on setting up a mini business plan for your Portfolio Career. Finally, I've included some notes on keeping really useful data on your clients and a few thoughts on terms and conditions, otherwise known as 'the small print.'

SURVIVAL CHECK-LIST

Let's start by assuming the worst and list the things you could do right now if you really had to, in order to create an income. First, please list the things you have been doing to earn money to date and put your gross income against each. If you've been doing one job, list that and your gross salary. Please note against each, on a scale of

1 to 10, how easy it would be to pick up those earning activities again, even for a short period. Easy is high, difficult low.

Now for an honest assessment of the minimum expenditure you can get away with financially – your basic needs. So please list all your expenditure. Everything, even simple inconsequential things like newspapers or chewing gum. Then we'll start peeling away the layers of 'wants' to get to the core 'needs'. Use the proforma below, filling in the 'Item' column with a brief description (eg 'mortgage' or 'dog food') and putting the figures for it in the 'Cost' column. It may help you to 'bunch' or categorise items of expenditure but it's not essential. You'll probably find it easier to use a month rather than a year. Once you've made your list, add up the total expenditure and then use columns 'A' and 'B' on the right as follows:

1. Decide which of your expenditure items you would include on an 'absolutely essential' list. You are only allowed to select

ESSENTIALS LIST			
Item	Cost £/$	A £/$	B £/$

60% of the original list. When you've decided, put a line through the items you've discarded. Now move the *figures* for the items you've kept (your essentials) into column 'A'. Add the column.

2. Repeat the process, eliminating a further 40% of what you thought were essentials. Move the *figures* for what's left into column 'B' and add them up.

It's a strange and uncomfortable feeling, isn't it, peeling away all those essential inessentials? How close did you get to the real boundary between your 'needs' and your 'wants'? It is remarkable how little we need when things are really tight and it's good to have a notion of what we'd let go in an emergency.

Next we'll look at what you *propose* to earn and spend in your new business. This is a lot more cheerful.

CASHFLOW PROJECTION

Now I know this is going to seem like hard work and really boring, but it is essential to have an idea of where your money is going to come from and go to – and what's going to happen if more goes out one month than comes in. If you don't know, you are out of control. Then, if you are out of control and things get tight, other people will take control for you. People like your bank. Friendly as they may be, they will have an entirely different agenda from yours.

It seems so obvious but, in my experience, not everyone has a cashflow. But, once they get hooked and realise how incredibly useful it can be as a planning tool, they never look back. It's not difficult and nowadays you don't even have to do the maths; there are numerous software programmes that will prepare your accounts, calculate your tax and produce cashflow projections before you can say: 'overdraft'.

The cashflow projection proforma below is set up in such a way that you can check your predictions every month. There are 'projected' and 'actual' columns. As each month goes by, you can fill in the actual income and expenditure next to the projected and, gradually, your forecasting will get more accurate. You'll learn to allow more time for a particular client to settle bills, for example, or to predict more accurately your stationery costs. To begin with, though, be very conservative as far as your income is concerned

99

(that way, it can only get better) and be rather generous with your projected expenditure. I'm not encouraging you to be profligate, simply to allow enough leeway so there are no nasty shocks later.

You will notice that the bottom line of the cashflow proforma is called a 'running monthly balance'. This tells you at any time what you'll have in the bank. You can see ahead to lean moments and fat moments. If it looks as if, for example, September is going to be an income disaster area, you can plan ahead to redress the balance by working out what you'll have to: invoice in July (assuming 4 to 6 weeks to get clients' cheques); do in terms of actual work in May and June; and secure in the way of new business in April. On the other hand, if it's likely that November is going to be a brilliantly abundant month cashwise, plan to buy that new computer then. This is the beauty of the cashflow. (At this point I'd like to point out that I don't normally get excited about accountancy matters, but I do know that this simple planning procedure works.)

The cashflow projection will help with your tax planning too, so have it ready to show your tax advisor if you have one.

A final word on cashflow projections: yes, I agree, they are 'guesstimates' and the data you put in them will change but don't worry about the inaccuracies – they will sort themselves out as you develop your business and begin to establish earning and spending patterns. Generally speaking, at the beginning you'll know better and more precisely what your outgoings are likely to be than your income. I believe this is the right way round anyway as it gives you an incentive to work to a target.

MINI BUSINESS PLAN

I always wonder when giving workshops or business advice why people cringe so much at the idea of doing a business plan. It is essential and one of the most useful things you can do for your business. Perhaps it has to do with the preconception that business plans have to be great fat tomes in order to be 'proper' – they don't. Perhaps it's the common perception that they are very complicated and have to be written in some incomprehensible business-ese – not so. As far as I'm concerned, the thinner and simpler the better, provided they have made you cover all the ground.

The important thing to remember is that you are not writing your business plan for anyone else. You are writing it for you. So write in

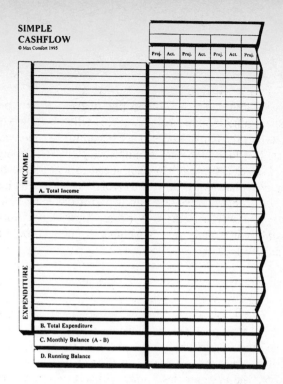

SIMPLE CASHFLOW
© Max Comfort 1995

		Proj.	Act.	Proj.	Act.	Proj.	Act.	Proj.
INCOME								
	A. Total Income							
EXPENDITURE								
	B. Total Expenditure							
	C. Monthly Balance (A - B)							
	D. Running Balance							

a way that *you* can understand. There is this myth that business plans are written to impress (or convince) your bank. They may be used for raising a loan but they are primarily compiled to guide your business through its development. The one person your business plan needs to impress is you – you'll be putting a great deal of energy into following it.

So the business plan should be a working document, something you carry around with you in your briefcase and something you constantly refer to and refine, not something propping up the coffee machine in the corner. It's your plan of action for developing and implementing your business idea. It plots where you are now, where you want to be in – say – two years' time and, therefore, how you get there.

Finally, and perhaps this is where some of the reluctance stems from, business plans are not solely about money. To be sure, it plays a major role but also key are the ways you market your product or service, the ways you maintain quality, the simple procedures you propose to adopt to get the business running smoothly and the most important aspect of all: your personal visions and objectives that the business is intended to deliver.

The headings and notes that follow are how I normally set out business plans but please rearrange them in whatever way you feel best serves you. Fill each section in but don't feel you have to start at the beginning and determinedly work your way through. That's the hard way. Start where you like or where you feel confident and build out from that point. And don't think you have to do it in a hurry. Take your time and leave lots of gaps between working on it, because while you are out enjoying yourself or digging the garden and not thinking about it, the Business Plan will be forming itself in your sub-conscious, ready for the next session.

Try to be as brief as possible. This is a working document, not a novel.

Your Present Situation
- What you do now, your range of skills and/or products (see Skills List in Chapter 4).
- What is good about your present situation.
- What is not so good about it.
- Why you want to change.

Your Vision or Great Idea/s
- Where you want to be in seven years' time – personally (check your Visions List in Chapter 4).
- Where you want to be in two years' time – with your business. This is what's known as your 'mission statement'.
- What inspires you?
- What is it that you are going to offer (your products or services). Describe their essential features, not every little detail – that comes later.
- What is so unique about them? (List at least three 'unique selling propositions' (USPs) for each product or service.)

The Market for your Great Idea/s
- Who needs your products/services? Is there really a need out there or is this just something you'd like to do or make, a nice idea? This is important, so be horribly honest with yourself.
- What sort of people/companies are they?
- Where will you find them?
- What factors will make them want to buy your products/ services? (Don't forget, very few people buy on price – watch a good second-hand car salesman at work if you don't believe me.)

- Apply the 'so what?' check ('My widget's the most colourful widget in the world.' 'So what?' 'My widget has bigger knobs.' 'So what?' 'My widget will cost you 20% less to run than other widgets' 'Now you're talking!')
- Who else is operating in your market?
- How well are they doing?
- What are they charging their clients?
- What's so special about their product/service?
- Are there any gaps you could fill, any opportunities only you could exploit?
- What's likely to happen to your market? Read up on trends in the business pages of your newspaper. Inform yourself on the way things are going. Now may not be the best time, for example, to set up a company making LP racks for record stores.
- Having done the above, do you want to modify your products/ services? If so, now's the time.
- Now would also be a good time to do a SWOT analysis on your business as you'll have the market details fresh in your mind. See Chapter 4 for the one you already did.

Your Strategy for Delivery
Having decided what your products or services are, that they are needed and at whom they are targeted, you now need to work out how you are going to deliver them. In order to put yourself in the position of your intended clients, recall the times that you've bought services or goods. When were you really impressed or seriously underwhelmed? Why?

- How will you let the market know that your products/services exist? Word of mouth, networking, multi-level marketing, advertising?
- How will you sell your products/services? Will you do the selling or will you get someone else to do it for you? (This is critical as most people believe they hate selling, forgetting that this is exactly what they are doing most of the time anyway. If you remember that most people 'buy' people first and then what they offer afterwards, you can see that every chat in the pub at lunchtime is a form of selling yourself.)
- Having made the sale, how will you deliver the products/ services?

SIMPLE TIME TABLE

Action/Task	Year 1997 — Month FEB		MAR					APR	
Week	17	24	3	10	17	24	31	7	
Getting Office									
Family agree on spare room	■■								
Order new phone line	■								
Source Desk		■■							
Order desk			■						
Paint Office			■■						
New carpet					■				
Move into Office					■				
Move Dog out!					■				
Build Kennel for Dog!						■			
Put shelves up							■■		
Getting Equipped									
Buy new computer					■				
Buy new filing cabinet					■				
Get out Answerphone					■				
Check on Mobiles						■			
Fix coffee machine						■			
Phone installation				■					
Other Preparation									
Business Plan						■■■		■	
Cashflow Forecast						■■■			
Filing !!!				■		■	■		
Source Filing clerk									

- What quality procedures will you adopt and for which aspects of your business?
- What kind of after sales service will you offer?
- How will you treat your customers? How will they experience your services? What will be your policy on complaints, for example? Recall the different ways you've been treated when you've bought something: was it a pleasant experience or were you treated like a nuisance to be got rid of as soon as possible? Could you trust the person delivering the service? If so, why?

The Crunch

You've thought about it. Now it's time to time plan your implementation. This is the scary bit because it has to do with commitment. Yes, actually doing it.

So you need to draw up a simple timetable like the one above and list all the things that need doing to get your business going, in the order that you need to do them. This is your Action Plan, be as detailed as you can. Against each item put a line that goes through however much time you think will be needed to complete it. So, if you believe you can carry out the kind of market research we talked about above in two weeks, put a line across the two weeks you've selected. (By the way, I'd use pencil, not pen, if I were you.) Be realistic and remember those 'shoulds'.

This is also the time to work out your costs – how much will it cost you to produce the goods? Don't forget simple things like delivery/transport costs. (As an architect, I always had to remind myself, for example, to warn clients that my fees didn't include the fees payable for Building Planning Approval.) So don't overlook the 'hidden' extras and then end up paying for them out of your profit. If one of your portfolios is actually making things and you buy in raw materials, be very aware of the cost trends of those materials if you're going to have to hold *your* prices for a while. Ask anyone in the paper industry how crucial this is. There'll be more on how to charge for your services in Chapter 12.

Having worked out your costs compare these with your business's basic financial needs. Is there enough profit margin? If not, re-examine those costs, check what others are doing and review your financial needs.

Keep a careful record of all your calculations – you may need to refer to them in a hurry so the clearer they are the better. You don't want to find yourself with your financial facts down around your ankles when you're in front of a customer who's about to sign a deal.

Yes, it is essential to do a cashflow projection for your business. If it's very similar to the one you've already done, that's fine but maybe you'll want to tweak it in the light of your market research. Whatever you decide, it has a very important place in your business plan.

Preparing for Action
You've committed to doing it, you've planned it out in detail. Now you need to let everyone know what you're doing, how brilliant it is, how exciting. (Don't forget to *be* excited.) Make use of your contacts to spread the good news.

Draw up a list of people you need to tell and decide too how you're going to tell them. Some will expect a phone call, some a call with a follow up letter, others will be best advised with a letter. Very special people will merit lunch. Decide what it is you want them to do for you. Some will be mentors, advisors, some will be influencers – well connected people who can mention your name in the right places – and some will be networkers. Mark against each person which category they come into and then design the most effective approach. It helps to recall how people approached you and how you reacted. How would you do it better?

Now you've prepared your business plan, reach for a glass of something restorative. Then *read it*. I know that sounds obvious. You'd be surprised how many people don't. In a week's time, read it again. Alter it, add to it. It's easy enough with a PC. Remember, it's a working, living document, one that adjusts to changing circumstances, that adapts to new demands.

STAYING ON TOP OF YOUR CLIENTS

This is clearly the best way round – you need to maintain an accurate and regularly updated record of your clients because the more you have and the greater the variety of services you provide, the more complicated it gets. To stay sharp and to know exactly what you've done – or contracted to do – for whom, it's essential that you have the data at your fingertips, wherever you are. If a client calls you on your mobile phone while you're on a train trundling through a remote peat bog and you have more information on the project you're doing for him than he has – right there with you – well, you can guess the reaction.

On the subject of database systems for computers, these are being augmented, upgraded and superseded all the time so spend some time on getting one that serves you. It pays to list manually exactly what you want it to do and then, and only then, go to see a few software houses and insist on precise answers. Also, insist on plain English; jargon is so often a convenient way of not telling someone something, of ducking an issue. Remember, too, if your manual systems don't work, they don't stand a chance of being computerised efficiently.

You will want to avoid having to input information more than once but you may well want it – or some of it – to go to more than one location in your database. This is where relational databases come into their own. Be very clear with your computer salesperson exactly what you want and how relational you want to be – now and in the future. Exactly. And expect to spend a lot of time in the store.

In the various architectural practices I worked in, the data was arranged with the client or project as the central focus as we nearly always provided different services for different clients – unlike a factory making roof tiles and supplying them to different customers, in which case the product would be the central focus and the database organised accordingly. We had separate job numbers for each project and the system, if maintained on a regular basis, worked well. For portfolio working, I suggest adopting the same approach as architects and make the client the focus – it's a good model to work to, in any case.

You may already be set up with a database on your PC so go with that. The list below does, however, cover the scope of information you should have at your fingertips and which you should be able to download as a 'quick reference' information dossier, in hard copy, for when you go visiting.

CLIENT CONTACT SHEET

- Client's name and business name.
- Client's addresses; phones, faxes, e-mail/internet numbers.
- Close contacts in company: names, direct lines, mobile phone numbers, home numbers, home e-mail/internet, address etc.
- Personal details of close contacts in company: source of introduction, personal quirks and preferences, important family details (eg about to have a child, recently left partner, anniversaries etc). How much you refer to or act on this information will depend on your relationship with the contact and where you got the data from.
- Contact record – every time you write or call, note the simple gist of the communication (eg confirming change in specification for widgets or advising change of meeting venue). I cannot overemphasise the importance of this kind of record keeping, particularly if you ever have the misfortune to be sued over something or if your client is being sued and you can help him or her with the case by corroborating with your records – brilliant for client loyalty.
- What the client company does or makes – a brief description of each would be useful.

- What you believe the client organisation needs and what you may be able to sell into it.
- Approximate client company turnover and profit last year.
- What you have already delivered to the client and the response/feedback.
- What you would do differently next time if anything.
- Dates of invoices sent by you to the client company.
- Payment record including whether they are 30, 60 or 90 day payers (essential information for cashflow projections).
- Other suppliers you know they use and for what.

It need hardly be pointed out that some of this data is likely to be sensitive so the more sophisticated your database, the better. You should be able to restrict access to some information and select particular areas – or fields – to work with for specific tasks. It would be embarrassing, to say the least, if your client company's turnover appeared on the address label for their Christmas card. You may laugh but stranger things have happened.

TERMS AND CONDITIONS

I don't know about you, but I hate and mistrust those poorly printed and tiny, tightly packed paragraphs on the back of order forms or other such documents. Have you noticed that they're nearly always printed in half-tone? I feel I'm either being browbeaten by the sheer weight of the words or I'm about to be 'had' if I sign. Most people I know cross their fingers and sign anyway. If they do read the 'small print' it's usually so badly written or wrapped up in legalese (some would argue that the two are synonymous) that they give up, none the wiser.

I have a very simple set of terms and conditions, designed to inform rather than confuse and which spell out clearly what I will be doing for the client and what I won't. I list the range of services I can provide and those I can't. I state very clearly indeed that I cannot accept responsibility for decisions affecting the project which are taken without my knowledge or with which I disagree. I state that all decisions reached between me and the client will be confirmed by me in writing and only acted upon once the client has signed them off.

My fee structure is explained openly in terms of the alternative ways of paying, standing order, lump sum, hourly etc but I do not publish rates (see Chapter 12, Financial Footwork). I insist on a purchase order from large organisations.

I invite clients to raise questions around my 'small print' as this encourages debate and clarification.

The size of *my* 'small print' is exactly the same as for my correspondence – that is, not small at all.

I feel comfortable knowing I have nothing to conceal, my clients feel comfortable with the very up-front way I treat them and everyone gains.

I would, however, strongly advise running your terms and conditions past a legal advisor before you issue them, not to complicate them but to check for anything that might leave you exposed. Do try to resist the temptation, however, to fall-back into legal jargon.

Chapter summary

- Writing a Survival Check-list – the bare minimum you need to get by.
- The importance of setting up a cashflow projection so you can plan ahead for success and avoiding problems.
- Writing your mini business plan – a document slimmed down for easy and effective use, by you, not fattened up to impress the bank.
- The importance of knowing more about your clients than they do – keeping really useful records that you can have with you at all times.
- Preparing a set of terms and conditions that don't confuse and obscure but reflect your straightforward, up-front attitude to doing business.

PART THREE
PORTFOLIO CAREER
MAINTENANCE

This part of the book is intended to perform two functions: for those contemplating a Portfolio Career it goes into more detail of what to expect and how to deal with it; for those already embarked on their Portfolio Career it serves as a series of reference points against which to check how it's going, as a refresher and as encouragement. Some readers will find some of the advice so obvious as to be mildly irritating. I make no apologies as I have seen some dreadful situations in my time, situations that arose because someone overlooked the obvious. The obvious can be dangerously invisible.

[The global society is going through a time of transition] when it seems that something is on the way out and something else is painfully being born. It is as if something were crumbling, decaying and exhausting itself, while something else, still indistinct, were arising from the rubble.

Vaclav Havel, Philadelphia, 4th July 1994.

Chapter Seven

What's going well – what's not going so well?

An opportunity to review the progress of your Portfolio Career or to learn about some of the pits before you fall into them.

During the years I have spent in the West, I have been surprised to discover that many people seem willing to accept a way of living that is not deeply satisfying. Starting in childhood, they grow used to operating at less than peak effectiveness. Without even realising it, they cut their own energy, dull their intelligence, and undermine their own best impulses.

Tharthang Tulku: 'Mastering Successful Work', Dharma Publishing 1994.

Although this chapter is primarily for those almost or already in a Portfolio Career, it would be an interesting exercise too for those in full time employment or fresh out of it. Try testing some of the issues highlighted against your situation; you might be surprised.

   It's also likely to be a valuable resource for those who are faced with dealing with Portfolio People, with managing them or working alongside them.

SO HOW ARE YOU FEELING ABOUT YOUR PORTFOLIO CAREER?

I've picked out some of the more common responses at Portfolio People workshops to the questions: 'What are the good things about your Portfolio Career?' and 'What are the not so good things?'. Read them through and list on your pad those that apply to you too.

Good things

'Choosing not to do something if I don't want to.'
'Meeting different people.'
'Doing the things I love best.'
'Variety!'
'The sense of freedom.'
'There's plenty of stimulus.'
'Never being bored.'
'Being in control.'
'Being responsible for my own life.'
'Being "institution"-free.'
'Making lots more money.'
'Being appreciated and valued.'

Not so good things

'Not having enough money.'
'Home being 90% about work – my office creeps into every corner.'
'Worrying about what the next steps are.'
'Financial and other fears (eg failure).'
'Not having a central focus.'
'Managing priorities.'
'Explaining what I do to people who think I'm an eccentric dilettante.'
'Over-commitment and worrying that there's not enough time to do it all.'
'Motivating myself and standing on my own two feet after being in a corporate environment.'
'Time management.'
'Loneliness.'

How did you fare? How many 'goods' did you score and how many 'not so goods'?

What would you add to either list? Make a note on your pad. Be specific. For example you might add:

– feeling motivated in the mornings and bouncing out of bed;
– having a sense of purpose and direction in my life;
– feeling really good about myself;
– seeing more of my family;
– being bored;

– waking up more tired than when I went to bed;
– sinking enthusiasm;
– wishing there were clearer boundaries between my work and my family life.

Now go back in your pad to your Visualisation List, your Abundance List, your List of Gifts and your SWOT Analysis (Chapter 4). Look to see if there are any obvious connections between these and the list you've just completed. For example, you may have 'a tendency to let awkward situations go unchallenged' in the W of your SWOT and worry over the lack of boundaries in your home affecting your work. Or you may link 'your intelligence' from your Abundance List with feeling respected and valued. What exactly is the connection? Identify too which are quantitative issues (mark these 'A') and which are qualitative ('B').

Having identified the 'not so good' issues, how do you feel about them? Do they feel insurmountable, manageable or not too much of a problem? If there is fear around any of them, go into the fear and find where it sits.

What about the 'good' issues? Pause a moment to acknowledge and appreciate them.

Take as much time as you can over this reviewing exercise and contract with yourself to do it on a regular basis.

So, how do you feel about your Portfolio Career now?

ARE YOU STILL GIVING YOURSELF A HARD TIME?

Are you still playing the 'I'll look at it over the weekend' game? Why? Have you taken on too much? Do you need to? Do you really 'look at it over the weekend', or just rather guiltily late on Sunday night? If you do have to do some work at the weekend, that's fine but treat it as a temporary situation and do it openly and without resenting it. It'll get done a lot quicker.

PP Tip: Write a review day in your diary for two months from now and contract with yourself to honour the commitment to do it. (Have you noticed how the things that always get scrubbed out or moved in our diaries are what we have agreed to do for ourselves, whether it's the filing or going for a swim? What is it

115

that causes them to be scrubbed out? Fear of offending someone, excessive eagerness. Don't we count too? Or perhaps there's some lurking 'avoidance' there.) If it helps, get a good friend to agree to be present at your review – preferably well away from home and office – and to make sure that you do it.

If you consistently find yourself working at weekends, look at how you use your time during the working week. Chapter 8, Time Management, will help with this.

FEARS AROUND MONEY?

How's the income? Do you feel you need more? Please revisit the section on Survival at the beginning of Chapter 6 and then ask yourself the questions:

- For what do I need more income?
- What could I bring into my life if I had more income?
- What could I bring into my life without more income?

If you're really struggling with the bills every month these may seem like daft questions. They may, but they will briefly focus your attention and energy out of the fear around your lack of funds and into a bit more objectivity. Even if you rant and rave at the absurdity of the questions, you will be releasing some of the pent up frustration.

Next make a list of all your most profitable *and* enjoyable activities, even the one-offs. Go back for at least 12 months.

Now ask yourself these questions:

- What can I do right now to increase my chances of a better income?
- What is preventing me right now from increasing my chances of getting a better income?

If nothing comes up in response, don't worry. Forget the questions for a while and return to them later. Then try again.

The answer may be really complex or really simple. Be prepared for either.

CLIENT MAINTENANCE

What sort of client/customer feedback are you getting? What's your client turnover rate? How long do they stay with you?

You need to be asking yourself these questions on a regular basis, particularly if you feel you should be getting more clients. Chapter 11 on Relationships will help but in the meantime consider this question: 'How well are you serving your present clients?' I believe there is a definite connection between how you treat your existing customers and the number of new ones you attract. Remember me in my freezing yoga class? If you are putting all your energy into worrying about getting more customers and not enough into looking after those you already have, it will show. Your body language, even your voice over the phone will subtly convey that anxiety. Anxiety is not attractive – and your existing clients are not blind either; they will notice your worrying and start to question the reasons.

So, what's the answer?

Focus on your existing clients and giving them the best possible service in the world, and your knowing that you are doing something really well will bolster your confidence in yourself and your service. As a result, your behaviour will become attractive again, your voice over the phone will convey confidence, reliability and trustworthiness. People will want to do business with you.

I'm often told by clients that they are too busy to market themselves. They are full of work and enjoying the buzz of deadlines and heightened creativity. 'Marketing? That'll have to wait until we get a bit of time, until the pressure's off.' Yet, impossible as it may seem to put into practice given the time constraints, this is just the time to market yourself. When you are busy. When you are fully self-assured and experiencing the adrenaline rush that comes with success. Because then you will be oozing confidence, you won't be cast down if a job doesn't materialise and, above all, your lack of fear will be extremely attractive in a business world full of it. Who would *you* rather employ: someone who is clearly timid, uncertain and very needy or someone who feels really solid, someone you could rely on?

SPIT AND POLISH

Now let's look at what else you could improve.

117

SPIT & POLISH				
Activities	How good am I at this?	Feedback	I like this'	Could do better

Complete the checklist above, being as specific as you can.
Start by listing all the things you do in the course of your work, even
supposedly trivial things like filing. (If you need a memory jogger,
go back to your seven-hour itch exercise in Chapter 4.) Then, in the
column headed 'How Good am I at This?', give yourself a score
between 1 and 10 (good is high) for how well you do the particular
task. So, if you're absolutely brilliant at making the coffee, give
yourself a 10. (If you're doing it ten times a day, maybe you should
score yourself 2 for avoidance.) If you are a tip top presenter, score
yourself accordingly. Now, in the column headed 'Feedback', score
yourself between 1 and 10 on the basis of feedback received from
clients, colleagues, friends and family. Where there's not been any
feedback, enter a 6. Next, in the column headed 'I like this', enter a
1 to 10 score on the basis of how much you enjoy doing the
particular task, with 10 being for most enjoyment. Add your scores
horizontally, entering the results in the 'Could do better' column.

How did you get on?

If you scored 25 or more you've nothing whatsoever to worry about for that task.

20+ is good but keep an eye on it.

15–20 is not very good – put a large asterisk next to it.

10–15 is awful – another asterisk please.

10 and under – well, a triple asterisk on this.

Now cross out all the items without asterisks and focus on those with. Then turn to Chapters 8, 9 10 or 11 for specific ideas to help with tuning up your activities and addressing these problems.

Chapter summary

- Listing and reviewing the good things about your Portfolio Career.
- Listing and reviewing the not so good things about your Portfolio Career.
- Getting into the habit of regular performance reviews – how do your clients experience the service you give them?
- Being honest about your fears around money.
- What you need to do to increase your chances of a better income.
- Looking after your clients – actually doing 'let's do lunch'.

- How well do you do all the jobs, large and small, in your Portfolio?

Chapter Eight

Time management – beyond the Filofax

Putting lots of appointments, action points and instructions to yourself in your personal organiser, electronic or manual, is fine – but not enough. You actually need to do it as well and that's a bit more difficult, hence the title of this chapter.

We are speeding up our lives and working harder in a futile attempt to buy the time to slow down and enjoy it.

Paul Hawken in 'The Ecology of Commerce'.

Work has become a health hazard. More than 80% of employers say their workers suffer stress, while heart attacks are most likely on a Monday morning – on the way to, or arriving at, work.

Nick Williams, writing in the 'Daily Express' March 19th, 1996.

TAKING THE ROLLING PIN TO TIME

Do you recall the Tale of the Magic Fish, which time and time again allowed itself to be caught by the fisherman so he could make ever more grandiose requests on behalf of his insatiably ambitious wife? Having started with a hovel and progressed to a palace, it all went terribly wrong when the wife wanted to be God and they got their hovel back.

We're the same with time. We surround ourselves with labour-saving gadgets which do in seconds what a few years ago would have taken days. Our microwave ovens 'bake' potatoes in minutes, our faxes transfer documents that before would have taken days in the post. Our washing machines free up Monday mornings. We don't even have to make pot of tea any more – we put a tea bag straight into the cup. In theory, we're saving huge amounts of time.

Yet, somehow, we never seem to have enough of it. We're so busy spending time trying to create more time for ourselves that we never have enough time to enjoy what time we have.

It feels to me like a particularly vicious cycle with all the intelligence inherent in a circular travelator. As Hawken says, it's futile. You'll never catch up. If, as I pointed out in Chapter 5, we also spend large chunks of our time trying to be in the past or the future, we can't experience the time that's right here – now.

Needless to say, we are time obsessed. I have never really understood the attraction of getting to New York two hours quicker by taking Concorde, unless it is to impress the neighbours. I would much prefer to get there slower – and enjoy the process. Why is quicker better? What do we gain by doing or getting things sooner? And what do we lose from it? For me a recent advertising campaign for British Rail food sums the issue up nicely: 'Snatch a snack', they exhorted, or 'Grab a bite', as if there were no time for actually tasting the food; eating had degenerated into something akin to shovelling coal into the boiler to make the train go faster.

Try this. Find a bridge over a motorway somewhere, a bridge with a pavement you can stand on, and just stand on it. Watch the traffic pounding along beneath you. Isn't there something rather absurd about all that restless roaring and rushing? Where are they all going – and why?

We are somehow made to feel, particularly in a business setting, that we have to squeeze every last drop out of our time, the company's time and, in consequence, the world's time. As a result, what's happening is that we are all rushing faster and faster towards our own demise. Is that what we really want? I thought the idea was to live longer and, as the saying goes, whoever heard a man on his deathbed wishing he'd spent more time at the office?

Portfolio People, in the busy pursuit of their polymorphic careers, are more susceptible than most to the pull of time. Time management is the burning issue on all the workshops I run. The great fear is that there's not going to be enough time to 'do it all'. There's a lot of pressure – from fear or curiosity – to pack more in, to achieve more, to stretch time out as thin as possible, to increase its coverage. Never mind the quality, feel the width, as the catch-phrase goes. That's the problem – quality. Which is why it's very important to regularly ask ourselves the question: why are we in this Portfolio game?

Before you read any further, go back to the Visions List you completed in Chapter 4 and read it.

Now this is all very well, I can hear you think, but in the real world we have to choose between deadline and breadline. Perhaps you do. But it might be easier to bear the pressure if you know why you are doing it. The following will help too.

THE POWER OF POTTERING

I have discovered something I call the Power of Pottering. When I have a long list of things to do and when they are particularly or potentially boring administrative jobs that I'm really not looking forward to, I sometimes abandon any idea of doing them in order or, more importantly, of finishing one before I start another. It sounds like a recipe for disaster and complete chaos but in fact it works very well. I don't invest anxiety in sticking to the list or to completing it, I allow myself to flow through the day without any 'shoulding'. I follow my fancy and enjoy a thoroughly unstructured and seemingly undisciplined time, drifting between one incomplete job and another.

In going to fetch one thing, I'll see something else that needs doing – it may not even be on the list, but this doesn't matter. I'll stop what I was doing just before and get into the new task. Filing flows seamlessly into watering the plants and jotting down some ideas for a presentation next week; sorting my receipts in preparation for doing accounts becomes a minor reorganisation of the archives and making coffee turns into writing letters. As a result, I am really relaxed, the tasks don't feel nearly as burdensome *and* they get done. Suspend the linear, rational mind for a day and try allowing in enjoyable mayhem. That's the important thing: it's enjoyable.

While we're on the subject . . .

FILING FOR FUN

This may seem a strange idea to bring into a chapter on time management until you reflect how much time many of us waste looking for things and, generally, how little time we devote to putting them where we – or others – can find them easily. Some of us operate a piles filing system and a few of us actually file in filing cabinets. Which scheme do you tend to operate?

Under the piles system, you end up with the table (generally the dining room one), shelves, desks, sideboards, sofas and carpet completely covered with shaky stacks of paperwork, likely to collapse at any moment. It works reasonably well for those whose constructions these are, since they can usually remember in which stratum some document or other was deposited. Where the system falls down is if anyone else wants to find anything, the cleaner decides to have a purge or you rather rashly invite people for dinner. Once those piles are moved or even – God forbid – amalgamated, everything is lost.

The filing cabinet is a great improvement but, beware, although it may feel very large when you are dragging it up the stairs for the first time, once you begin to rather enthusiastically put files in it, its limitations become only too apparent.

In either case, the important thing to remember is that, contrary to common practice, filing is not really intended to be a form of delayed waste disposal. Those drawers, files and boxes are actually for 'live' stuff we need to have handy at all times. Instead they seem to fill rapidly with all sorts of things that, in the light of day (usually a day many months later when we're desperately looking for something vital), we cannot believe we didn't throw away.

The problem is, filing is boring – and challenging. You have to make decisions about where things go, what to keep and what to bin. Do you know anyone who actually likes filing? I remember, when interviewing once for a new, high-powered secretary, deliberately talking up the more exciting aspects of the job like arranging my travel or going to conferences and desperately talking down the onerous bits – like filing. Especially filing. It felt as though the very mention of the word would drive away even the most conscientious candidate. A newly self-employed client of mine confided recently that she had no idea how tedious the filing was – hitherto she'd had a personal assistant to 'do all that stuff'.

This is the nub of it. We see filing as a second class activity to be carried out by someone else if possible, certainly not by us. Can you imagine a library where the books never got put back on the shelves? It wouldn't stay in business very long. Your record keeping is no different.

If you really can't bear it, there is a solution: get a friend to help, ideally someone whose discretion you can rely on as they may come across personal stuff. Invite them over for a Fun Filing Day, provide a meal and make sure you have a good bottle of wine. You'd be surprised how quickly it gets done when there are two of you. You might even enjoy it.

Why would they come? Remember curiosity? You can return the compliment later – and satisfy yours too.

Strange as it may seem, I've done 'fun filing' over the phone, except in this case it wasn't much fun and there was no wine. A client had telephoned in deep despair at the growing piles of paper in her lounge and was lying in bed not knowing what to do. I talked her out of bed, into her dressing gown and through to the kitchen. There 'we' made her a cup of tea. I then talked her into the lounge, told her to select the first pile her eye lit on and take it back to her bedroom for sorting. She was able to get through it quite quickly, partly because I was there to encourage her but partly too because it was only one pile. The sight of paper everywhere in her lounge was so awful it completely paralysed her will.

By breaking up a huge, seemingly insuperable task into small, manageable pieces, it becomes possible. There are so many things which never get started – let alone completed – because we see them as a mountain rather than as a pile of stones. Pick out the stones – the parts of the task – which you feel most able to tackle and keep your target to completing only those parts. The rest will follow in good time.

As a Portfolio Person, it's vital that you can get to your records quickly so regular filing is essential; not only to absorb new material but, particularly, to filter out old and redundant stuff you no longer need or which can go into archive boxes. Try and have a regular, weekly filing session. You could do it to coincide with a good radio programme, so you get your reward *and* you don't feel guilty for listening during working time.

PP Tip: An important point here: never throw anything away that may have a bearing on your ability to prove a financial transaction, like receipts or purchase orders. Keep *everything* to do with money. Archive it if you like, but do keep it.

Here are a few further points on record keeping that will serve you well by saving time.

• Use colour coding for different clients or jobs. It's much easier to recognise files through colour than through words which you actually have to read. The London Underground system uses colour to subliminally guide passengers from one line to another and all the exits are ringed in yellow. You can adopt the same simple but very effective principle.

- Start modestly. You don't need to establish a complete filing system with lots of different files for a job that's only just begun or which may not go any further. One file will do fine, and you can always expand it later as necessary. Use files that you can open up easily to access that stuff right in the middle, otherwise retrieval will be a chore and you'll either get irritated or lazy.

- Your filing system will probably divide into two sections: jobs and maintenance. Below is a list of basic files you'll need to get going. As they fill, divide them up and create more.

  - bank statements;
  - bank correspondence and copies of forms, agreements etc;
  - bank reconciliations;
  - invoices in;
  - invoices out;
  - petty cash;
  - accountant;
  - tax – returns and records;
  - tax – correspondence;
  - lawyer;
  - copies of non client-specific legal agreements;
  - correspondence with suppliers;
  - correspondence with consultants;
  - brochures on services and products (eg office equipment);
  - hard copies – data base;
  - hard copies – other.

- Give each job or client an individual number which should be used on all correspondence and other documents, including invoices. This way, your filing will be so much easier, you'll find things faster and your clients' administration departments will take you seriously. Each client should have a file to him or herself. That way, you can take it along to meetings without the need to cover up any bits that have to do with other clients. People are naturally quite curious as to who your other clients are and all you need to do is go to the washroom for a moment.

125

- Are you one of those people that does things right away, to get them out of your hair? Or are you someone who puts things to one side, to be done 'later'? The problem I've found with the 'later' method is that by the time 'later' comes, you've probably forgotten a lot of what you were going to do. It's therefore a more difficult task and your feelings of frustration gang up with the fact that the novelty's worn off anyway. Result: you put it off to 'later' again, you start worrying and what was once something you were excited about becomes real drudgery. Added to which you've probably got another pile on your carpet. It's not easy, but try doing stuff as soon as you can – you'll feel a great deal better for it because you won't be carrying all that guilt around with you.

THE WEEK IN 3/2 TIME – THE DOING/MANAGING DUET

Of course, all this talk of filing and administration – pottering or otherwise – is fine but what you should really be doing is the work that earns the fees, that creates the income, isn't it? 'Admin' must take second place. Or must it?

Consider what would happen if you drove your car continuously and never put oil or water in it or had it serviced. It would soon seize up and grind to a halt. It's the same with your business. However much pressure you are under to do the actual 'work', if you don't maintain your business regularly, it too will grind to a halt. So getting the right balance between doing and maintaining is crucial, particularly for Portfolio People who rely on everything being just so, where it should be, at all times.

When I was at school I played the violin, not well enough to be noticed but not badly enough to be overlooked completely. Consequently I was always in the third violins, the orchestral equivalent of the third team reserves. The *raison d'être* of the third violins was 'scrubbing': providing a continuous and hopefully harmonious background for everyone else by frantic bowing on a very limited range of notes – a bit like the drone of a set of bagpipes. There was one piece of music that was always in demand at garden parties and church fêtes: Mozart's 'Eine Kleine Nachtmusik'. I think he must have had a grudge against third violins, because it contained more scrubbing than any other piece I ever played. So there we were, bowing arms a blur of high speed musical monotony, hating every minute of it, while the first violins played all the interesting bits and got all the admiring glances from the old ladies. The point was, without our humble scrubbing, those stringed prima donnas of the vicarage lawn would have sounded as thin as the cucumber in the sandwiches.

Maintaining your business can sometimes seem as tedious as that scrubbing but without it things can get very one-sided and eventually break down. Striking a balance between the bits you really enjoy, that give you a buzz, and the boring bits is quite hard, so I have a suggestion.

This may alarm some people, but I believe the ideal we should be aiming for is a week where three days are spent actually doing the fee earning, productive work and two days spent maintaining our business and ourselves. This, to my mind, is a business in harmony with itself. Gandhi would agree: he recommended a maximum four hour day.

Having alarmed some of you, I'm now going to challenge you. I'd like you to conduct an experiment over the next week. It will take a little time and I am relying on your complete honesty. It's this: I want you to keep a careful record of your activities over the week, a time sheet if you like, a record of everything you do. Include all the time you spend making tea or coffee, filing time (I'm sure you do *some*), time having lunch, productive/working time, invoicing time, time spent travelling, time spent thinking or day-dreaming (both are very important, as we'll see later), contacting time (letters and phone calls, especially chats with friends) and time spent looking for things. The chart below will help. Be as detailed as you can. The point of all this is to discover how much time you already spend on maintenance, on so-called 'non-productive' activities. I think you'll be surprised.

Add all the hours in the maintenance columns to get a total for maintenance time. Now do the same for the productive time. Finally, work out the ratio of the two. For example, if you did a total 55 hour week and, in that, 34 productive and 21 maintenance hours, your week will have had a ratio of 62% productive to 38% maintenance, equivalent to about three:two of your average 11 hour days.

If your ratio is four productive:one (or less) maintenance, you need to ease up on yourself. If it's two productive:three maintenance it sounds as if there's too much of that scrubbing.

Of course every week will be different. There will even be some eight day weeks. 'Even?' I hear some of you think. That's the beauty – and the challenge – of Portfolio Working but it does help to take the odd 'snapshot' of your working habits, if only to remind you of how wonderfully you're doing.

I mentioned chatting on the phone with friends. This can be delightful and dangerous. Delightful because it's so much more enjoyable than working: dangerous because you can spend an awful lot of time doing it and end up working into the night to catch up with yourself. You need to state very clearly that you are working, you'd love to talk to them but could they phone back in the evening on the home number. Say this a few times and the word will go around – and don't give out your work number to people who are likely to ring up to tell you all about their holiday, bar by bar, beach by beach, conquest by conquest. If, on the other hand, a good natter is going to make a difference to the quality of your day, go for it and enjoy it without feeling guilty.

ACTIVITIES RECORD/TIMESHEET		
Activities	Maintenance Time	Productive Time

BUNCHING

If your office is in the north of the town – be it London, Los Angeles or Sydney – and you have two or three clients in the south, it makes a lot of sense to arrange meetings with them all on the same day. If I'm not careful, I could end up spending huge amounts of time on unnecessary travel. It can sometimes take me longer to get across London than to get deep into the countryside outside. So I do my level best to 'bunch' my meetings in a particular area if I can. I also try to work out the quickest and most efficient route for the day, arranging the appointments with the absolute minimum of travelling between venues.

This can sometimes mean being very strict with clients. The temptation, particularly with someone you really want to impress, is to drop everything and say you'll see them any time. Don't.

There are two good reasons for this.

First, is the client likely to be impressed by someone who is instantly available? What kind of message does that give them? If the boot were on the other foot and you were the client, wouldn't you be more reassured by someone who was in demand? So, play a bit hard to get – in the nicest possible way. If you're busy doing your accounts on Thursday or you're with someone else, say you have a meeting or make great play of being helpful and finding an alternative time. Usually, if you rehearse your day or your week over the phone with a client, they'll find a slot that you've also got free *and* they'll be impressed with how busy you are. Of course, if it's absolutely vital to them that you be there on Thursday, then let the client know this is a concession in view of the urgency. (But beware. Do remember my architectural clients and my 'ever-ready' team standing by to perform miracles overnight, because miracles have a habit of becoming commonplace if repeated too often. And who is it that has to keep pulling those rabbits out of the hat? Right. Make sure you don't run out of rabbits.)

The second reason is this. I've already said that one of the most important aspects of having a Portfolio Career is managing your precious time effectively. So, having carefully constructed an impressively seamless sequence of important events for the next week or so, why mess it all up because someone else hasn't got their time management as well sorted out as you. Bear in mind that it's not pushy clients that will sabotage your carefully laid plans. It will be you: *your* anxiety and *your* eagerness.

129

Just in case, though, however skilful you may be at 'bunching' your meetings, don't pack them in too tight. It's a good idea to allow some slack in between. I try to add at least 15 minutes to all my travel times in order to allow for meetings running on, delays on the train, hold-ups on the road, essential phone calls at pre-arranged times, not finding anywhere to park or a coffee break.

In order to bunch your meetings effectively, you'll need to know which clients are likely to go on beyond the agreed time. So you'll need to have agreed a time and be clear about keeping to it.

You'll also need to be adept at getting around town or country with the minimum of aggravation. Here are some thoughts on getting more out of your travelling time.

ZEN AND THE ART OF FLYING CARPET MAINTENANCE

As a Portfolio Person it's not going to be just a case of getting from A to B. More like A to Z, via every other letter in the alphabet. You will sometimes spend serious amounts of time on the move.

I need to sound a little note of warning here about something I call the Travelling Trap. It's very easy to get hooked on mobility, to mistake frantically rushing around from place to place for being busy and productive. All your energy will go into the rushing and not into the doing. Slow down for a moment and consider what it was that you were actually trying to achieve amidst all the bustle.

So how do *you* get around at the moment? Do you mix 'n' match, different ways for different days? Trains for out of town, buses or 'the tube' (subway, for my US readers) in town, taxis? Or do you resolutely take the car everywhere?

What are your needs while travelling? Apart from getting quickly and safely to your destination, do you need to prepare for your next appointment? Can this be done in your head or must you have your briefcase out or your laptop computer going? Perhaps you need to make some notes from the meeting you were just in, while things are fresh in your mind. Difficult to do in the car – unless you're in a particularly good grid-lock. Do you need to carry awkward heavy stuff around with you?

Since you will need to arrive at meetings in the best possible frame of mind, consider which mode of travel you find most conducive to being that way. How do you arrive – cool or hot? Are you calm in the car or do you regularly experience rumblings of road rage and arrive fuming and in a foul mood? Is the train best for you or do you hate being stuck with a lot a people you don't know and locked into someone else's timetable? Like me on occasion, do you take a taxi for the last stretch in order to arrive composed and in control?

Consider for a moment what your travel needs are, as opposed to your travel habit. List them and also the sorts of journeys you make regularly. Tick the journeys you really enjoy. What does this tell you?

Personally, I'm a great believer in trains and taxis for long journeys and buses and the underground for short excursions. I easily get bored with studying other people's rear bumpers, even if they are travelling at 70mph. Train travel means I get more than a few fleeting sightbites of the landscape flying by, I can enjoy the whole view, do my work or day-dream (more on this later) and there's usually a refreshments trolley. Also, it's a lot easier to sound convincing when making excuses for arriving late if you can put it down to the train rather than the traffic.

Whatever your mode of travel, you'll need to stay abreast of the infrastructure. If you're a driver you'll be aware of the gradually slowing speed of traffic, certainly in town, and so the more contingencies and alternative routes you know the better. Keep aware through the radio of what's happening but, above all, make sure your mobile phone is charged. Best of all, have one of those chargers you can plug into your car's cigarette lighter, and charge it as you go.

If you prefer to take your chances with the transportation system, arm yourself with timetables, route maps, connections maps and essential phone numbers. Don't just rely on the normal route from A to Z. Have some alternatives up your sleeve because you can almost guarantee that if there's a cancellation or breakdown it will be on the day when you absolutely have to be at Z on time. In London I have to contend with security alerts, daily jams and the continual rebuilding of large parts of our underground railway system. I am used to finding alternative ways around the blockages, like water around rocks. I know my patch.

Arriving on time for a meeting, and in a good mood, depends on being well-organised beforehand. It may sound obvious, but having the correct address with you helps. Also try and get as detailed instructions as you can, or even have them fax you a map – don't be afraid to ask. Most people love to give directions. It's amazing though, how some of us just point our noses or our cars in a vague general direction and hope.

To paraphrase a famous saying, it is at least as important to travel pleasantly as to arrive.

However, should you be unlucky enough to be stuck in a 20 mile tail-back with ten minutes to go or in a train which has just ground to a halt in the middle of nowhere, there are two things you should do. First of all: breathe. Deeply. Panicking isn't going to help. Then call your appointment and explain the situation. You could have part of the meeting over the phone. That way, even if you never get there, both of you will have the feeling you've achieved something.

Assuming you do arrive, there are some useful rules around arriving for appointments.

MEETINGS: ALWAYS LATE OR SOMETIMES EARLY?

You will have noticed that some people are always late for meetings and some – but not so many – are always early. Some people are late for some meetings and not for others. So what's going on? Being late for meetings is generally experienced as a lack of respect, an absence of commitment or just plain pathetic. The recently collapsed Barings Bank had a reputation for keeping even its most important visiting clients waiting, suggesting that the clients were lucky to be there at all. This was simple arrogance. I believe there are also those people who get a buzz out of the drama of arriving late, sweeping in like Elizabeth Taylor at the Oscars. It only works once, in my experience. People remember.

How late is late? Five minutes or 15 minutes? Usually the answer depends on what kind of meeting it is and who's going to be there. Most people are reasonably tolerant, especially if they've been warned that you're running behind.

PP Tip: People don't arrive late for meetings with someone they're a bit scared of. If there are a lot of people to be convened, and you want to ensure the meeting starts on time, get that person to arrange it.

My rule is always to assume that a meeting will begin on time, and try to arrive promptly. That way, I show proper respect for the arrangement – and, more importantly, *I* don't worry.

On the other hand, there's nothing more infuriating than someone arriving early while you're still going through your preparations for the meeting or trying to finish something else off. In my experience, those few minutes between meetings are often a frenzy of focused activity. Interrupt at this time and you'll be deeply unpopular.

Those that arrive early for meetings are either terribly anxious about lateness or terribly well organised. (You, of course, will be in the latter category.)

If you've arrived early for a business meeting you can either sit in your car, go for a coffee or announce yourself to the receptionist, explain that you're early, please not to disturb your contact and 'would it be OK if you waited in the foyer?' Generally this goes down fine, you might get a coffee and you can spend the time calmly preparing, reading your notes or looking through the company's Annual Report so you're even more knowledgeable and impressive when you eventually go into the meeting.

What do you do, on the other hand, if it's your meeting, the coffee's getting stewed and the visitors haven't arrived? Stew with the coffee? Although I never tell this to people who come late, I relish the extra moments it gives me; I make phone calls, I do some writing and I definitely drink the coffee. Also, as far as I am able, I stick to my 'meetings rule': we've agreed a certain amount of time so that's what they get. No extensions. The only exception to this rule is if I'm really enjoying the meeting. This sounds a bit selfish but it's practical and keeps the boundaries around my time firmly marked out.

Quite often, people who perceive they have the upper hand, whether they are clients or not (like Barings), will expect others to be on time but will feel quite comfortable about keeping them waiting themselves. Depending on the circumstances, you should never wait longer than 30 minutes for someone visiting you unless you've had a message to say they're delayed and on their way. If *you* are visiting and are kept waiting, always check carefully with the receptionist to see if they've actually told your appointment (or a secretary) that you're there or whether they just thought they had. If, despite messages, you are kept waiting with no reasonable cause or apologies given, tell the receptionist you'll call again later and then leave. Avoid waiting longer than 30 minutes. To do so makes you seem far too eager and, moreover, rather lacking in confidence. In any case, do you really want to deal with someone who is so arrogant? Barings' clients had only themselves to blame.

DREAM TIME

By now you will have noticed another alarming tendency of mine, which is to imply that day-dreaming is to be recommended. It most definitely is. Taking time out, playing hookey from yourself, is essential business practice. Why do you think my ideal week has two whole days for maintenance? Well, in your business, what is the most valuable asset and one that needs regular maintenance? Right. You. When I recommend to clients that they take one day a week entirely for themselves, to do with what they will, they look at me with disbelief – and longing. Going for a walk (yes, for a whole day), sorting out your stamp collection, reading a good thriller or just lying in bed pondering on the meaning of life, all these are terribly important.

If I were forced to say what the most important message for Portfolio People was, I would say without hesitation, 'taking enough time for self'. And the more pressure there is on your time , the more 'self' time you need to take. It sounds absurd, but it works, if you let it.

If we all did more day-dreaming, for example, we would stand a better chance of getting the absurdities in our lifestyle into some kind of perspective. If we're constantly chasing our intellectual tails, we don't give ourselves a chance to stand back and observe ourselves and our circumstances objectively. By taking our minds 'off the hook' and allowing in a little aimless day-dreaming, we give the rational mind a vacation from its hamster-wheel. While we do the dishes or watch the wind in the trees, the random thoughts that wander through our consciousness are actually performing a valuable function for us, in spring-cleaning the tired corridors and letting fresh air into our brains. The result: we return to our tasks refreshed and alert, often with surprising new insights into a problem or state of affairs that was bothering us only a few minutes previously.

So if you find yourself feeling physically or emotionally tired, or (especially) when you're feeling that there simply isn't enough time to do all the things you've got to do, stop a while. Just stop. Take time off. Go and look out of the window. Take the dog for a walk. Do your laundry. Allow the passive mind free rein, and let some of that stress and anxiety drain away.

RING FENCING YOUR TIME

Making time to allow the process of day-dreaming entails you being protective of that time. It will be under siege from clients, from colleagues, from friends and from family – and from you. So establish routines if you can as they are the easiest way of protecting any special activity. Dieting in a haphazard fashion, dipping in and out of the regime, is not nearly as effective as sticking to a set routine. Family and friends can help you protect your 'me' time. Tell them about it and explain why you need it, that it's not about you trying to play truant or get away from them, but about maintaining yourself and being a nicer, more balanced and more successful person as a result.

Of course there will be times when you will break the routine. Try explaining to a new client that you can't see them next Friday because that's your 'lying in bed all day' day. But be aware that it is a concession and try to find some compensating time. If you can't manage a whole day – and it is hard – try for half a day or even a couple of hours. If you can really forget your business during that time, you'll feel so much better.

I'm often asked about weekend working. Well, it depends on your circumstances. If you are in a relationship or you have a family, weekends tend to be sacred. If not or if your partner or family do other things at this time, and if you feel inspired to do some work, then do it, but do have some time in the week for 'just being'. Also, if you are going to work at the weekend, do work. So many people play the 'I'll do it over the weekend' game and never actually get round to it. They get to develop a debilitating sense of non-achievement and other people can suffer too. One of my worst nightmares was having only four weeks to prepare a competition entry for the design of an incredibly important building for the centre of London. This happened because the senior partner at my firm of architects had said regularly every Friday afternoon for about three months: 'Oh, don't worry, I'll do it over the weekend' and never quite managed it.

135

ELASTIC TIME

Shakespeare talks about time travelling 'in divers paces with divers persons', of ambling, trotting and galloping time – and time standing still. Make sure you get a good mixture of all kinds of time and experience its elasticity. When you are doing something you don't really enjoy and you manage to put your energy into it, time will go by fast. If you hate every second, you'll experience every second, one after the other, slowly.

Sometimes, inevitably, circumstances and deadlines will conspire and you will find yourself in a very tight corner – possibly two of them at once. I would like to be able to tell you that Portfolio People have an effortless way of solving this, but I can't. We may be almost superhuman but as far as I know we have not yet mastered paranormal time. There are only two possible ways of getting round this one: bluffing it, or laying your cards on the table.

By keeping very quiet about a problem, you can sometimes 'wing it' successfully, but your anxiety levels will be getting dangerously high and you may not be very good company. On some level, someone will probably guess that all is not well.

Honesty is probably a better policy, so where feasible, you should tell the parties all clamouring for your attention that there is a problem and why and that you can't do exactly what they want exactly when they want it. If you have a good relationship with them they will be understanding, particularly if you can use your imagination and prove that doing it a different way will serve them even better. If the person you've double booked doesn't know you very well, that's the one not to let down.

It's time at last, I think, to talk about diaries.

THE DIARY – A PORTFOLIO PERSON'S BIBLE

One of my favourite secretaries used to joke about my diary when arranging meetings for me. She called it The Bible. She was not far wrong. I followed it religiously.

As a Portfolio Person you need to treat your diary with all the respect due to a good friend. Handled properly, it can be a third hand, helping you keep all those balls in the air. Misused, it will paralyse you while you watch all the balls tumble to the ground.

Diary maintenance is an art that has to be learnt. The best example

I can give you of imaginative and effective diary use is that of a *maître d'hôtel* running a busy restaurant frequented by the rich and famous. Imagine the complications: Lady So and So has to have her regular table come what may but the *maître d'* has no idea when she will turn up; a member of some royal family arrives amid tight security and everything has to be turned on its head to accommodate him and his bodyguards; the restaurant is full but one of the world's great film stars won't take 'no' for an answer. All these problems have to be sorted out without any of the other guests realising that anything is amiss.

At times you will feel like the *maître d'*, basically under siege from the glitterati wishing to reserve a table in the limelight. Every time you enter something in your diary you are reserving your time. With a client, a colleague, a team member or yourself.

So how do you manage? With great diplomacy and by knowing pretty well in advance what is likely to happen. Just as our *maître d'* will have a sharp sense of precedent and pecking order – and know who can be put off or kept waiting and who not – you will know from your experience and relationships with your clients what they are likely to demand and how many of their demands you must accede to. Where he will always have a table or two 'on ice' and will keep his ear to the ground for news of regulars arriving in town, you will keep some 'daylight' in your diary for the unforeseen arrival or request – it may look clever to have a solidly booked diary but actually it's pretty stupid. Be prepared, like your *maître d'*, to accept the unexpected gracefully.

The skill in managing a diary effectively, and not being tipped into chaos by someone else's demands, is in being very, very realistic. It is really knowing your own strengths and weaknesses when it comes to delivering the goods, and not making wild promises. It is in understanding your clients and their time-keeping habits.

As I have already said, it's also about sticking to your boundaries. Like the number of tables in the restaurant, your time is finite – and *you* can't spill out onto the pavement. There will be times when you'll have to take the 'risk' of saying no. The person you've just put off for a week may not be very pleased but they will respect your steadfastness. After all, would they want you to blow *them* out in favour of another client?

This is an area where relationships – good relationships – are crucial (see Chapter 11).

137

A few other hints:

- Although a great deal of my work is done in groups and teams, I always try to keep at least one day a week unfettered by meetings of any kind so I can respond in an emergency. If it's not taken up, that's great, I get some time for me.
- I also try to get meetings for ongoing projects established on a regular basis, same time every week or month and, preferably, same place. This helps the other participants who, it should be remembered, are also struggling with wayward diaries, and it particularly helps me.
- If I can, I always take the initiative in meetings for setting next meeting dates and I try to get as many booked as far ahead as I can. That way I get them when they suit me.
- Be aware of the realities of your body clock, the times when you feel full of go and when you feel flat. Track your daily rhythms, note the times when you are alert or tired, when your motivation sags or you can't wait to get on with everything. Does food make you sleepy, like it does many other people? Are you a cockerel or an owl, best first thing in the morning or late at night? Once you know the location of the peaks and troughs in your energy, plan accordingly. If you like big business lunches, don't schedule too many meetings afterwards and do fix important meetings at your peak energy periods.
- Diary reviews are important. Every month or so, go back through your diary and see how it went, with the benefit of hindsight. Where were the difficult moments, when did it all go smoothly and why? This will give you useful pointers for future diary maintenance.
- I always keep a note in a corner of my diary of how many hours I have spent on a particular project. This is obviously an essential daily routine if you are charging your clients by the hour or day but it's also a useful record which enables you to check your fee estimate with actual time expenditure. Rather like your cashflow forecast with its projected and actual columns for each month, it will help you avoid quoting too low and losing money or quoting too high and losing the job.
- If you are using a manual – as opposed to an electronic – diary, make sure it's big enough. A page a day is essential.
- It's good practice to keep a back up copy of the crucial contents of

138

your personal organiser. (Have you ever met someone who's just lost theirs? You'd think there had been a death in the family.) Don't, however, run two diaries simultaneously. There is a temptation to have a slim line version with you and a desk version back at the office. This is fatal. You need all the information with you at all times and you certainly don't want anyone else organising your time. Nor do you want two diaries leading separate lives of their own. A slave can only serve one master.

- Always use pencil to make manual diary entries – and always carry an eraser.

One thing you should try to do now is draw up a simple but flexible timetable, not as a rigid regime never to be varied, but as an indicator and structure to guide your meeting making and your time use. The one below is an example.

TIMETABLE FOR ACTION

Start by copying it and using the copy to plot out what a typical week looks like at the moment. Then check for successful bunching, excessive travelling or erosion of your time by people persuading you they are more important than you. What do you see in your

		BASIC WEEKLY TIMETABLE					
	Mon	Tue	Wed	Thu	Fri	Sat	Sun
Morning							
Afternoon							
Evening							

139

week? Resolve or weakness in the face of the time bandits after your most precious resource? Enough or too little time for maintenance and for you? Be honest and then use the original to plot out a week that might serve you better.

A final word on time. In the next chapter we'll look at focus and commitment. How well you manage these two crucial aspects of your Portfolio Career will depend largely on your time management skills. So, before you read on, review quickly the key points in this chapter.

Chapter summary

- Magic fishes, fishermen's wives, Concorde and tail chasing.
- Spending more time on making less time.
- Portfolio People's susceptibility to the pull of time.
- The quality versus width battle.
- The Power of Pottering – shelving efficiency for the day.
- Fun Filing – piling or filing, long-term waste disposal and filing with a friend.
- Tips on paper management – colour coding, starting modestly, numbering systems and the 'doing it later' game.
- The week in 3/2 time, making time for maintaining your business – and you.
- Bunching appointments and being firm with clients over making meeting arrangements.
- The A to Zen of Mobility, the Travelling Trap, finding the best ways to travel, what to do if everything grinds to a halt and getting to know your patch – and other people's.
- Being late or early for meetings – how to deal with transgressors and how to operate yourself.
- The vital importance of day-dreaming – letting your passive thoughts clear the way for objectivity and understanding.
- Protecting your most precious asset – your time – from others and from yourself.
- Experiencing and utilising the elasticity of time – speeding up slow, boring tasks, slowing down those which are too fast and dealing with time clashes.
- Diaries – learning the art of managing them like a *maître d'* in a top restaurant, being firm about your boundaries and leaving daylight in your diary.
- Taking the initiative in arranging meetings so they suit your

needs, knowing your body clock and when not to arrange appointments, reviewing your use of time and keeping records of it.

- Creating a simple timetable which serves you well.

Chapter Nine

Focus and commitment – staying still in a whirlpool

We are taught to expect novelty almost as a right. If it's new and improved, it's got to be better. Consequently our attention is often on the new, the latest, the trendiest. The dangers this attitude can hold for Portfolio Working are spelled out in this chapter.

I was giving a lecture in German and, after telling two funny stories, began to wonder why I hadn't produced even a flicker among my audience. Then I realised I was giving the wrong presentation, in the wrong language – to a group of Americans!

I'm not so much a Portfolio Person, more a portmanteau person.

Portfolio People workshop participants.

We have already established that you are sometimes going to be faced with making difficult choices when managing your time and your diary. Unless, like me, you do most of your work in a meeting or workshop environment, you've also got to allow time for the work itself – and you will inevitably experience being pulled simultaneously in different directions when doing it. Most of the time it will not be clashing clients tugging for your attention. Most of the time it will be your commitment, your focus and your enthusiasm that creates the multiple polarisation of your energies.

When a great number of different events are happening around you it can be hard to hand out attention and goodwill evenly. You may have clients who shout louder than others, who are more difficult or who you are rather nervous of. The temptation will be to give more of your attention and time to them and to neglect those who don't jump up and down so much. Or it may be that one client is paying a lot more than another or buying more of your time than others. Will he or she get more of you, pro rata, than the rest? It would also be silly to ignore the fact that we are often more fired up about new projects than existing ones.

These are issues you need to be keenly aware of and keep a continuous eye on, because . . .

A CLIENT IS A CLIENT

Have you ever experienced being put in second place in no uncertain terms? Having the amount you spend with a company clearly determine how you are treated? You can hear it in the voice; it's either respectful and seriously attentive or – after being kept hanging on for a long time – it's nakedly condescending. I'm reminded of that wonderful scene in the film 'Pretty Woman' where Richard Gere takes Julia Roberts shopping in Beverly Hills and demands thousands of dollars worth of obsequiousness from the practically genuflecting shop assistant.

If you, as a client, phone someone only to be told, 'He can't speak to you at the moment, he's preparing for a client. Can I get him to call you tomorrow?' how do you feel? In the first instance, I would imagine, rather rejected and very annoyed. In the second, quite determined to take your business elsewhere.

Clearly, you don't want that to be *your* clients' experience. Whatever they are paying you, they are a client. In his autobiography, Peter Caddy, former Commanding Officer in the RAF and co-founder of the Findhorn Foundation in Scotland, tells a story from his days in the catering business. When a 'down and out' left the tea-room after nursing a single cup of tea for the whole afternoon, the manager of the establishment insisted on opening the door for him and thanking him for his custom. Whatever his appearance or his background, he was a customer.*

So resist the temptation to cut corners with 'less important' clients, to squeeze the attention you give them in favour of someone else. They may well come back for more – lots more. Or recommend you to someone, *if* they are pleased with the service they get.

Surprisingly, despite the spread of 'Quality Management' and 'Quality Assurance' schemes in the past few years, this realisation is still new to many businesses.

* *In Perfect Timing* by Peter Caddy, published 1996 by Findhorn Press.

You would do well to carry out your own 'quality' check. Examine how you perform the various functions of your business and how your clients may experience them, functions which include easily overlooked 'little' things like your telephone manner, how long before you return calls, the speed with which you reply to letters and the clarity and quality of your paperwork. Ask yourself if that's what you would like to experience as your client.

LEAVING THE LORELEI ON THE BANK*

You will also have to resist the temptation to 'put back' existing projects in your schedule in favour of newer, bigger or apparently 'better' projects – to abandon a carefully charted course in favour of other, more attractive clients who turn on the charm to persuade you over their way. This is not a good idea. It's the thin end of an awfully long wedge. Remember when the project you're about to jeopardise for a more 'exciting' one was exciting too? Express interest, leave a card and carry on. If they want you that badly they'll be back.

You may be trying to do a Ben Hur, driving three or more chariots abreast, struggling to maintain your interest and enthusiasm for all your projects and finding some of them becoming less than stimulating. Revisit the first excitement of those projects, the visions you shared then with the client. Look through your initial notes and proposals and recall the good feelings you had then. Remind yourself why you took on the project, what it meant then and what it has done for you since. Recall how it has served you, perhaps brought you to other things, to new contacts. Re-experience your gratitude.

This is not in any way to advocate turning down new work, but simply to encourage you to finish what you started and maintain your loyalty to your client – and his or hers to you. It is also to advocate keeping an eye on your needs, your needs to have that vital time to yourself, to have the time for maintaining your business that I spoke of in the last chapter.

So you *will* have to learn the art of saying 'not yet' or even, 'no

* The Lorelei is a steep rock on the Rhine near St Goar and the traditional haunt of a Siren who lures boatmen to their death with her beautiful song.

thank you' without actually saying it. If you must, stall: fix a meeting to discuss; ask the prospective client to send you background information on the project, that will take them a little time. Anything but slicing into time already allocated for your existing clients. Try to 'buy' time to finish what's on your desk right now before you turn that into a crisis by pushing it back, back to the limits of your endurance and credibility. Don't forget, as I've said before, that most people respect firmness, especially when it's clearly combined with a genuine desire to help. Most, as I say, would not necessarily want to employ someone who dropped everything to be with them in a trice – only to have the same thing done to them.

Don't let your eagerness to please or your enthusiasm for a new project knock you off course. You are particularly vulnerable to attractive distractions when you are bored or tired. Dare to be honest about your situation, principally with yourself but with a potential client as well. By all means be willing to find ways of answering their need, but not at your own expense.

There *are* 'emergencies', but check very carefully if that is what this is. Is it going to mean the end of Consolidated Amalgamated Inc. as we know it, if your review of their washroom signage policy isn't on the Chairman's desk in the morning? Find out first if the Chairman will actually be there in the morning. There was a time when I'd slave-driven my team to design a sumptuous palace for some insistent sheikh and spent hundreds of pounds to courier the drawings out to him for an immovable meeting, only to find he'd just gone off falconing in the desert for a month.

If it is a genuine emergency, remember that this is not your problem and then do what you can for them. What they want, more than anything, is cool-headedness and detachment, not another headless chicken. Remain calm and detached, but helpful. Keep your boundaries very clear.

Remember we talked in the last chapter about leaving 'daylight' in your diary? This is where it really comes in handy. If you've always got a few hours free here and there to play with, you can be the White Knight and go in with solutions and reassurance blazing.

If you really cannot fit in what is being demanded, keep the initiative by trying to find a colleague to help out. This way you keep the contact and goodwill of the client – and they are your client. See Chapter 11 on relationships and, particularly, networking.

Even when you are with your client, supposedly fully, 110% focused on their project, there is a danger that your concentration can sometimes waver. Those passive thoughts creep in and offer a few moments' of vacation from the matter in hand, or the excitement of a new project can creep up behind you and engage parts of your attention which should really be firmly present. You might simply be wondering what to eat tonight; or desperately trying to recall whether you fixed the hose on the washing machine before you turned it on this morning.

Your client may not be helping much. He or she may be wandering too, but audibly; or going over ground already covered; or waxing lyrical about those rubber grommets; or telling you something you've heard a thousand times before from other people.

So, in these circumstances, how do you stay focused? How do you maintain your concentration, listen effectively and bring all your experience and skill to bear on the matter?

The first rule of active listening is never to take your eyes off the person speaking, even if they're not looking at you. They will somehow know if you look at your watch or stifle a yawn, even if they are looking in the opposite direction. So don't let your eyes wander, because your mind will follow, right out of the window.

You do have to listen. So if it's getting really tedious, try to listen not just to the words but to the emphases, the inflections and the pauses too. They are telling you something. In other words see if you can hear between the lines. That way you will maintain your interest and also learn a lot more about your client.

Ask questions, it's a very effective way of breaking a monologue without appearing rude. It will also liven up the conversation and give you control. Tune in, if you can, to how they see things. Direct them with your questions. A very effective technique, beloved of some schools of psychotherapy, is to repeat the last word of the client's statement as a question. So if they say 'I'm really concerned about the way Tomkins is handling the marketing initiative, he doesn't seem to be getting anywhere,' the prompt, 'Anywhere?' encourages them to go deeper into the subject. This will give you further insights into the situation while, hopefully, helping them to get clearer in their mind about how things stand with Tomkins. Remember that when people talk, they are not just passing over information, thoughts or feelings, they are sifting, sorting, analysing and rearranging them too – for their benefit as well as yours.

Always take notes. It's a definite aid to concentration. When you get back to the office ... file them, right away.

Keeping focused partly comes with practice. With time, you come to trust that all the other balls will remain in the air while you concentrate for the moment on this one – that you will keep your footing in the whirlpool that you have created. Trust is something that we look at more closely in the next chapter.

Chapter summary

- A client is a client – treating everyone fairly and with equal respect.
- Doing a quality check on your business's performance – and yours.
- Keeping your excitement and loyalty alive for older projects.
- Standing firm when others are trying to knock you off course or entice you away.
- Balancing eagerness to please with honouring your needs.
- How to shine in emergencies and not even enter the hen house.
- Staying attentive among the rubber grommets when the world – and his dog – is playing outside the window.
- Using active listening to maintain your interest in apparently boring subjects.

Chapter Ten

Trust – Can I? Will they?

Doubt is a pain too lonely to know that faith is his twin brother.
Kahlil Gibran, 'The Prophet'.

WHO CAN YOU TRUST?

The first person you need to learn to trust is you. You need to trust that you will do whatever it is you've decided to do, that you will put everything you have into it and that, if it doesn't work out exactly as you'd hoped, you will put it down to useful experience and not sulk. You need to know the 'you' that you're going to trust.

This calls for a good deal of honesty, objectivity and pragmatism. You'll need to know what you can realistically expect of yourself – not just under the best possible conditions, but under the worst as well. You'll need to become very clear about your needs, and how they differ from your wants. Use the 'So what?' test on yourself, quickly check over your SWOT analysis in Chapter 4 and the assessment of 'what's going well, what not so well' in Chapter 7. Assess yourself as a parent would a child, with a mixture of love and patience, and develop a true picture of yourself, with all your good points and your not so good ones.

A CONFIDENCE CHECK UP

Having got as close as you can to an accurate, objective picture of you, now remind yourself of all the good things you've done. This we will call your confidence check up. Get out those testimonials – if they're not already up – study them and acknowledge that you did well. Open up your Compliments Book and say 'Aah!'

Confidence and trust have a symbiotic relationship. Confidence will give you the courage to trust; active trust will repay the compliment by endorsing and reinforcing your confidence.

Over time, you will learn that the more you allow yourself to trust, the more trust will work for you, in a very down to earth way. It will become a part of your inner stability, but it does require you to suspend your disbelief and test it out for yourself.

MEETING TRUST HALFWAY

Trust in yourself, and the power of trusting, is vital to Portfolio Working. On the emotional roller-coaster ride there will be times when you will be firmly convinced that your life is in ruins, that nothing will ever be the same again and that you are quite incapable of doing anything. However deep you sink into despair and hopelessness, that flicker of trust will help you up again. The stronger the trust, the quicker you will bob up. Having been down a few times and bobbed up again, your trust in the process will be stronger.

Bit by bit, you will learn to allow trust – in the form of a serene absence of doubt and anxiety – to carry you effortlessly through your complex working week. Riding the trust wavelength will help you over difficult territory and is an important part of your skills kit for designing a new type of working life.

It's important to repeat here the value of meeting trust halfway, of being proactively trusting rather than meekly patient.

It's not going to serve you if you set up your office, attach a brass plate to your door and then sit around waiting for a new client with lots of work to walk through the door. They may, but it's unlikely. You'd be surprised at the number of people I see who somehow believe that just by being available and skilled and nice they will magically attract clients to them. All their effort goes into arranging and re-arranging their office or their consulting room, not in finding people to give them business. Passive trust like that doesn't usually work, there has to be a bit of give and take. It's the difference between sitting under an apple tree, waiting for one to drop into your lap, or shaking the tree.

You have to do your bit. As Hippocrates said: 'Prayer indeed is good, but while calling on the gods a man should himself lend a hand.' So get on with all the tasks, see all the people, say what and who you are, clearly and without fear, and trust that you're capable of attracting work to you if you go out to meet it, that you will be able to make a magnificent job of it and that you will be rewarded well. Put trust to the test. Form a clear image in your mind of what it is you need and keep it there, trusting that you can attract it. See what happens. Expect a miracle. Try going through a day on the trust wavelength. I think you'll be surprised – and delighted.

Having said that, blind trust can be dangerous (and expensive), so meeting trust halfway has also to do with checking out who it is you're proposing to place your trust in. (Lawyers are an extreme form of this approach.)

Let's think about trusting others.

SWAPPING EXPECTATIONS

You will *have* to trust others. We do it all the time, like trusting that other drivers won't go through red lights. This is about social conventions and agreements, a kind of shared, tribal trust. Then there is the more intimate trust between two people doing business together. Here is where our individual, primal excitement response – be it fear or euphoria – lives, and so here also is where we need to be in touch with our instinctive feelings more than our emotions.

Trusting someone can be almost instant, on a feeling or hunch, but usually it grows in stages. There are innumerable little bits to the trust jigsaw: someone arriving on time for their first meeting with you; their body language, whether their handshake is limp or firm, how you feel about that; if they meet your eyes or not. (You can tell a great deal about someone from looking into their eyes.)

Later, liking may be confirmed through the 'feeling' that they're not concealing anything from you; the 'fact' that they did what they said they were going to do and did it on time; the 'fact' that they smile openly. As the relationship develops, there may be times when they do something extra for you, like introducing you to someone whom they realise you will want to meet. In a trusting relationship there is a strong element of supporting for support's sake. There is also an expectation that you can call on someone, that they will 'be there' for you, and vice versa. You are co-creating a mini tribe, pledged to defend and encourage each other.

Think now of three quite different people you trust. List in your pad the qualities in them that have earned your trust, the reasons you

150

feel you can trust them and how, in the past, they have demonstrated that your trust is well placed.

Now name three people that you know trust you. You should probably not include your children if they are young and you are still in the all too brief 'God like' stage as far as they are concerned. Do, however, include a member of your family, your blood tribe. What is it that you do and what is it that you are that earns their trust? Make notes.

Compare the two lists. Is there something they are doing to earn your trust that you could do for others? Or something you are doing that you'd like others to do?

Trust can be infectious. If you put your energy into earning trust, most people will respond. So, if you want their trust, demonstrate to them that they can afford to trust you. Very basic, terribly obvious but easily forgotten amongst the anxiety and fear of our prevailing business culture.

Then, of course, having earned the trust, you have to honour and maintain it. Like so many strong things in life, trust is also delicate. Once broken, it is hard to rebuild. So you need to work at it. If you wondered, a few chapters back, what all that maintenance time was for, all that day-dreaming, this is what it's for – pondering the intangibles in your business. If you let it, your mind will do the work for you while you are out playing tennis or bird watching. When, later, you need to make a decision around a trust issue, you'll probably find it's already made.

Helping the process along, as Hippocrates suggested, will be your intuition, if you let it. Intuition is a bit like one of those magic eye pictures with a hidden image – try too hard to see and you don't get it, relax and let your eyes glaze over and there it is. This is because the moment you try to make rational sense of your intuition, it vanishes. Accept it and allow yourself to enjoy the weird and wonderful things it brings to your attention, then it can work for you.

Take your intuition out on a test drive one afternoon, test other people for trust and reliability, test yourself, but do start with something fairly safe. Be modest – don't take risks. Gradually, as you become more comfortable with 'listening' to your intuition, you will develop trust in it and use it more and more. It's a powerful tool and you'll need it to develop the kind of relationships that really serve you.

We'll look at relationships in the next chapter.

Chapter summary

- Trusting yourself through knowing and loving yourself.
- A Confidence Check-up – dusting off the testimonials and reminding yourself how brilliant you are.
- Meeting trust halfway – shaking the apple tree rather than sitting under it hoping and waiting.
- Trusting others, what to look out for before you do and earning their trust, listing your trustworthiness and that of others you know.
- Trust maintenance – using your intuition to help you stay calmly alert.

Chapter Eleven

Relationships – growing your own Fan Club

The snow goose need not bathe to make itself white. Neither need you do anything but be yourself.

Lao-Tse

When considering relationships, let's start with the premise that we are all basically self-centered. There's not much point in beating about the bush. We all start out in life believing, like Galileo Galilei's tormentors, that the universe revolves around us. This belief system takes some pretty hard knocks once siblings appear on the scene or we go to kindergarten, but we hang on to the shreds of the illusion for much of our lives. It follows that in our relationships with other people we will be looking for what *they* can do for *us*. In a love relationship, there is an element of the other person reinforcing our self image, of helping us feel good about ourselves. In a business relationship, you might think, things are more straightforward – Company A has the rubber grommets and Company B wants them. End of story.

But is it?

As a Portfolio Person, your relationships are likely to be complex. They are certainly crucial. You'll need all the help and support you can get.

GROWING YOUR OWN FAN CLUB

So you'll need to spend time on growing a fan club – your fan club. People who will be rooting for you – but why should they root for you if, as we've said, they are essentially self-centered?

Answer: because either there is something specific they want from you or, better still, they like dealing with you. They will enjoy doing business with you if you give them that something extra: friendship, kinship, call it what you like. That something extra makes their day a happier experience if, into the depths of their drudgery, their boredom, their filing, you bring a sparkle, a brief moment of simple magic.

Why bother? Why not do the minimum necessary to get out of them what you want? After all, this is Business.

Two reasons. First, nearly all of us enjoy human interaction. We need bits of magic too. Especially if we're working alone and don't get to see friends and colleagues that often. Even if we never actually meet people, we can develop quite close relationships with them over the phone, fax or internet. Five minutes of friendliness, electronic or otherwise, can set you up for the day. Doing business should be enjoyable; we learn more about it and ourselves if it's fun and we're open, less if we are busy hating it and so shutting ourselves off. Being in touch, sharing anecdotes, swapping ideas and suggestions, even with someone on the other side of the globe that we're never likely to meet, is an essential part of business maintenance.

Second, we may need to suspend the self-interest arrangement and ask them to do something for us for no other reason than we need it – rather badly, preferably right now. Making sure your colleagues and contacts will do the impossible for you on occasion is a big part of developing portfolio relationships. If, for example, you are on the ropes with your cashflow (sound familiar?) and you really need an outstanding invoice to be paid quickly, you're much more likely to get Accounts at Amalgamated Consolidated Inc. to speed up the dispatch of your cheque if they know you and you've invested time in being friendly.

So invest. There will be times when you'll need to cash it in.

Plants grow towards the light, so be the 'light' in your business relationships and they'll grow towards you. You may have to make the first move, or even several moves. Try to engage the person's interest, locate their 'hot spot', ask questions about what they do and share a bit of yourself. It may seem like hard work with some people but, remember, if everybody else they spoke to today didn't make an effort, they are all the more likely to remember you. Be modestly and consistently proactive. Push the 'friendship boat' out a bit but don't try to occupy the whole pond. Avoid gushiness at all costs. Gush, and you'll begin to find that everyone is always 'away from their desk at the moment'.

154

WHO'S IN YOUR FAN CLUB?

Avoid being too selective – putting effort into some people and not others. Light doesn't discriminate between plants, you can't afford to either. In business, you have to be able to get on with some people, whether you want to or not. It's very easy to get hooked on 'glamour'. How many times have you made for the 'beautiful people' at a party and ignored the plainer guests, only to find out later that they are great fun? If you're doing business with someone, you need to get past the veneer, the image, and well into the substance before you finally make up your mind about them.

How do you get on with your business contacts? List them all, including among them your contacts at the bank and the tax office, your creditors, debtors, colleagues, suppliers, influencers, clients, cleaner, anyone you come across, however briefly, in the course of carrying out your portfolio of businesses. Now rate them for quality of relationship. The usual thing, 1 to 10, with 10 being good. If you've never spoken to your bank manager, give yourself a 1; if you're really pally with the Marketing Director of Universal Rubber Grommets Limited, give yourself a 10.

Select all the relationships you've rated 6 or under and note down why they've come in so low. The reasons may be simple, or more complex. Examine them.

Now make a list of all the people you would like in your Ideal Business Fan Club. Who have you included? The bank manager? Good. The tax office? Why not? In some ways, you need to spend more time on the people you feel less drawn to than those you feel a natural affinity with, because they are likely to be the ones you'll need to call on first in times of crisis.

One consideration: what would happen if you invited all your business contacts to a huge party with everyone you knew? How would they get on? Would they mix? Would you want to mix them with your friends? Sometimes we have to compartmentalise relationships, not only because some might not mix with others but because, for perfectly good reasons, we are different people with different people. Holding a conversation simultaneously with one of your most up-tight, teetotal and nervous clients *and* with your brother-in-law who revels in risqué jokes and gets drunk very quickly could be hard to handle. Who would *you* be?

You need to preserve boundaries between your business and home lives. They are very different for some, less so for others. Be clear where your boundaries are, how often you are prepared to make exceptions to your 'rules', let everyone know in the nicest way possible and then stick to them.

WHO'S WHO?

There are, of course, excellent reasons why we don't all get on with absolutely everybody. Personalities for a start. 'There's nowt so queer as folk' goes the old catch-phrase and we are all 'queer' in our different ways. So, being able to identify, and respond appropriately to, the different personalities you will come across can be very helpful.

There are many excellent systems around to help with this, some ancient and some modern. Hippocrates divided people into four types:

sanguine	– optimistic and cheerful;
phlegmatic	– slow and dependable;
melancholic	– sad and depressive;
choleric	– irritable and impulsive.

These types correlate with Hans Eysenck's personality types, sanguine corresponding with 'stable extrovert', phlegmatic with 'stable introvert', melancholic with 'emotional introvert' and choleric with 'emotional extrovert'

The more recent Myers Briggs Personality Types Indicators are particularly effective, so much so that they are now *not* used in recruitment. Companies who adhered too rigidly to Myers Briggs selection protocols found they were 'cloning' work-groups too narrowly, leading to serious communication problems between departments.

If you have the opportunity, it is well worth reading up or attending a workshop on Myers Briggs, but their system works by categorising people according to a number of different psychological types, initially identified by Jung and expanded by Myers and Briggs to include:

'E' Extrovert – people who are more focused on external events or . . .

'I' Introvert – those more focused on their inner world of ideas and experiences.

'S' Sensing – people who receive information through the senses and are realists or . . .

'N' Intuitive – those who are globalists, seekers of patterns and imaginative.

'T' Thinking – people who are analytical and who prefer logic or . . .

'F' Feeling – those who are sympathetic, compassionate and focus on values.

'J' Judging – people who love structure and order in their lives or . . .

'P' Perceiving – those who prefer to live in a flexible, spontaneous way.

From these eight characteristic types 16 personality pictures can be drawn and, using a series of psychometric type multiple choice questions, it is possible to establish very accurately and in some considerable detail what our personality type is.

My type, for example, is 'ENFP' which means I'm 'Extroverted, Intuitive, Feeling and Perceiving'. According to Myers Briggs, that makes me 'warmly enthusiastic, high-spirited, ingenious and imaginative'. I am also able to do almost anything that interests me and I'm quick with a solution for any difficulty and ready to help anyone with a problem. I often rely on my ability to improvise rather than preparing in advance and I can usually find excellent reasons for what I want.

Just before you begin to think I'm perfect, Myers Briggs also warns that, if not appreciated, my type can lose direction and focus, be easily distracted, become rebellious and ignore deadlines and procedures. If we're not careful, we ENFPs may neglect the details required for realising our inspirations, overextend ourselves, have problems saying 'no' to interesting possibilities and fail to apply reason and logic to judgements about people.

If I'm honest, this is pretty much spot on.

This is useful information as it points up, in an entirely non-judgemental way, our weaknesses and susceptibilities as well as our strengths. It helps us know what to watch out for, what situations to avoid and where we are likely to shine. Moreover, we can learn to recognise which type others fall into and plan and present accordingly. For example, a presentation to a 'Judging' type, and the materials that go with it, should be well organised and it should start on time. For a 'Perceiving' type, however, you will need to avoid giving too slick a presentation and instead be prepared to respond to the situation as it develops. Someone who is your 'opposite' (my opposite would be Introverted, Sensing, Thinking and Judging – ISTJ) would be a good person to run your presentations by before you make them.

If you are thinking about working closely with someone, it might be worth checking their type to see if they supply the opposites to your type and thus bring balance to the partnership.

Over the many years that Myers Briggs' methods have been used, some fascinating statistics have come to light. For example, someone whose type is Introverted, Intuitive, Thinking and Judging (INTJ) will more than likely be found in Scientific Consultancy, Financial Consultancy, Systems Design and Development, and Research Forecasting. INTJ types account for 1% of the population. Extroverted, Sensing, Feeling and Perceiving types (ESFPs) are the largest grouping in the population at 15%. Extroverted and Introverted types are split 75%–25%, as are Sensing and Intuitive types, while Thinking and Feeling are split almost half and half at 52% to 48%. Judging and Perceiving types are exactly 50/50.

In his phenomenally successful book *The Celestine Prophecy*, James Redfield talks about intimidator types, interrogator types, those who are aloof and the 'poor me's. He puts it down to the direct influence of parents and their type; aloof people, with their distant, unsociable nature, can infuriate others into being interrogators and intimidators create a 'poor me', defensive response in others. These responses quickly become habits.*

Knowing a little about body language is also helpful. Non-verbal communication transmits far more – and far more subtle – messages than words. Only 7% of peoples' perception comes from words. In a Senses Survey, it was established that Taste accounts for 1% of what we learn about others, Touch 1.5%, Smell 3.5%, Hearing 11% and Sight 83%.

So, for example, when the person you are regaling with the intricate details of rubber grommet manufacture begins to lose attention or get bored, they may well twiddle their thumbs, turn their head to one side every so often or straighten their trunk. They may prop up their head with a hand, lean back, stretch their legs, even

* *The Celestine Prophecy* by James Redfield, published in 1994 by Bantam.

close their eyes. Heaven help you if there's something lively happening outside the window – like clouds. *You* have to be the most interesting event in the room and your own body language will help here too.

Sitting absolutely still with only your mouth working is not really very visually exciting. I used to find that Danish TV news bulletins were the world's best cure for insomnia – the most exciting thing happening was the flicker. So use your hands to help make the point. I don't mean you should gesture threateningly at your audience or do an impression of early flight – but pointing at something to illustrate a point, and generally using your body to express your meaning, will help to maintain interest. If you can, stand up while you are making a presentation and move around as much as possible. Sales technique trainers recommend using a flip-chart, even if all you're doing is writing what you're saying, as not only does this 'anchor' the ideas in the minds of the audience, it makes for an interesting visual experience.

PP Tip: How to enter the room for a 'difficult' meeting or interview. Open the door, pause in the doorway for at least five seconds, slowly looking around the room and the faces, smile and then walk in, slowly. Very slowly. Imagine yourself as the President of the US or the Queen of England inspecting the Guard of Honour. Think regal. Feel regal. Be regal. Try it. You'll be surprised. So will they.

FAN CLUB QUALITY REVIEW

So, knowing a bit about your business contacts and how you rate your relationship with them, how do you think they experience their relationship with you?

Be honest, what could you do to improve their experience of you?

Check the quality of your service and your professionalism. How is it? Wearing a bit thin in the face of extreme pressure? Try to isolate why and deal with it.

Perhaps it's just a case of the relationship getting a bit tired, flagging. In need of an injection of enthusiasm or imagination. A client of mine was concerned about the 'feel' of his relationship with a major client of his. It all seemed a bit flat. He arranged for a little surprise at his client's pre-Christmas board meeting. With the help of an inside source, he secretly arranged for actors dressed as SAS combatants to storm the meeting and leave a pile of Christmas presents on the table. The clients were delighted at his sheer audacity and style and the relationship was revitalised.

I'm not suggesting you should now lay siege to your clients' offices but you do need to keep up the momentum of a business relationship. Traditionally, clients are 'rewarded' from a menu of junkets ranging from a drink in the pub at Christmas to a Ball at Henley with full regalia. A humble but good lunch is more the norm, but you actually need to have lunch – so many people say 'must do lunch' and then don't. Make sure you follow up on the idea; better still, make sure it's your idea. They may be thinking, just like you, that 'old so and so' never seems to be in touch these days, or 'I wonder what happened to that lunch we talked about?' So take the initiative, don't hold back. Even if there's no particular reason for meeting, meet. You never know. And treat it as an opportunity for subliminal networking, of which more later.

So far we've talked about relationships which are going reasonably well. What happens when they go wrong?

When things go wrong in a love relationship it's often an opportunity for growth; both parties can express, hear, accept and move on together, if they choose. It's not much different in a business relationship. You have a choice of getting on your high horse, trying to sort it out or skulking in a corner. If you want to sort it out it's a good idea to try to understand what the other party's agenda is. Also remember that fear – their fear – can be expressed as aggression, aloofness, rudeness and abruptness, so be patient. Don't just react to the surface expression, because the odds are that you'll be reacting to the wrong thing and you'll make matters a whole lot worse.

If your bank, for example, is saying 'no more cheques' and being unco-operative, you've either not been in touch with them enough, to keep them abreast of your situation and to state your needs or they've had a change of management or both. In either case, spend a moment working out what their needs are. Yes, *their* needs. They do have them. Mostly these days, they are to do with exactly following directives from on high in the banking structure, being able to understand information they receive from their customers and, you guessed it, hanging on to their job in the face of growing automation. You can help. Justify their existence, make them indispensable. Visit them, seek their advice and in the process get yourself out of a hole.

Speak to them and ask them what it is they need to get you a decision, how they would like it presented, what more they could do to help and then provide lots of supportive information which shows you are in control. Take the initiative. You will, of course, need to have your cashflow and other supporting data at the ready.

Don't ignore them. If you do they will soon be running your business and their policies won't bear any relation to those outlined in your business plan.

A client of mine got behind with the rent on his office. Terrified, he was preparing for the worst, just about to pack his bags and do a runner and hadn't dared to go near his landlord for ages. The landlord was fed up with what he perceived as my client's arrogance and high-handedness; he got angry enough to instruct lawyers. The client stood to lose his place of work and the landlord his tenant at a time when it was hard to let property out. By getting the two together and putting their respective cards on the table, we were able to agree a reduction in the rent and to spreading the arrears over a long period. The day was saved – just. The landlord got less rent but less rent was better than no rent; the tenant got to stay and put down a huge burden of worry and guilt. If they'd talked earlier . . .

It's the same with creditors. Talk to them, be honest and helpful and take the initiative in suggesting solutions. Remind them that a little of something is a great deal better than a lot of nothing.

If people are really insisting on playing heavy, remember: co-operate but do not comply. Things may be bad but that doesn't give anyone the right to walk all over you. Hold firm and display your resolution to resolve the issues.

Incidentally, it's worth considering that these situations should never arise if you keep your 'fan club' happy, informed and motivated to serve you, even in the direst circumstances.

Once a difficulty has been dealt with, don't think that's the end of the matter. Take the initiative again and discuss ways of avoiding similar problems in the future and generally better ways of working together. Show that you want to create something worthwhile from the experience, to build the relationship on the back of a shared problem and solution. Most people will be surprised as they are expecting you to slink away and lick your wounds, and never speak to them again. Surprise them.

Now you've got your fan club established and running smoothly, you'll need to add to it. Nothing ever stands still, least of all with a Portfolio Career. People will drop out, contacts will be lost despite your best efforts and projects will come to an end and need to be replaced. Everything will always be in a state of flux. This is why networking is so important to Portfolio People.

NETWORKING

Networking is not about selling your services. It is not to do with sending out huge numbers of flyers in the hope that someone will bite. Nor is it about advertising your services.

It is simply about being you. Being who you are and not what you think people want you to be. Being you amongst as many different people as possible. Talking about you and being active in listening to and appreciating others doing the same.

Because if someone likes you, they will want to buy from you, the next time they need what you have or do. You are your best marketing tool, so mix.

Above all, do not expect to get any work out of the interchange. In fact, decide positively not to. If you are standing there, glass of wine in hand, eyeing up the person opposite for fee potential, forget it. Your voice and body language will be flashing red warning lights. Their eyes will glaze over, they will escape at the earliest opportunity, avoid you like the plague for the rest of the evening and forget you almost immediately. On the other hand, if you see them as someone who is interested in you and what you do, nothing more, your voice and manner will be quite different, quite unthreatening – and they will remember you.

Remember, too, the power of listening and that people will be just as impressed by your ability to ask questions about what they do and then listen to their answers. Everyone enjoys talking about themselves. This is where your 'focusing' skills come into their own, particularly when there's a specially juicy conversation going on next to you and the person you're with is talking rubber grommets.

All this mixing will take time and effort, which is why I said you need plenty of maintenance time for your business. You also need to stay fresh and enthusiastic and curious if you're going to be a successful networker, and, as a Portfolio Person, very succinct. Pick your best portfolio to display, just as you would offer your best profile to a photographer. Be tantalising and intriguing. Let fall different tidbits into different ears. Enjoy it. Repeating the same story twenty times at a party could drive you to drink – or a full-time job.

Where can you expect to network? Anywhere. Dinner parties, receptions, meetings of professional bodies, clubs, on the plane, on the bus, in the washroom. So join as many trade and professional associations as you can, networking organisations and bodies like the Chamber of Commerce in the UK. Any place that will give you the opportunity to meet, mix and market yourself. And don't just join. Go along. I know people who never use the facilities they've paid for, as if joining is all that's necessary.

One major benefit from networking is that you get to meet people in the same boat as yourself and can share ideas and issues. Working for yourself can be a lonely business – you'll need all the support you can raise. You'd be surprised how many people are surprised to find they're not the only ones experiencing isolation. Many people's only experience of community now is through the work environment, rather than through traditional ways like the extended family or village. Networking is one way to turn the ghetto of solitary sole-traders into a neighbourhood of like-minded souls – in effect, even if not in geographical reality.

BLOWING YOUR OWN TRUMPETS

As well as getting along with people, you also need to sell to them. One of the numerous hats you will need to have in your props cupboard – and be prepared to don at a moment's notice – is The Marketeer-cum-PR Person. Promoting yourself well is about putting yourself in somebody else's shoes (including the editor of your trade magazine, or the prospective overseas customer) and correctly anticipating how they could benefit from what you are doing.

The first principle of PR is: never be afraid to pick up the phone (or write a letter).

The second principle of PR is: if it's a good story, someone will pick up on it.

The third principle is: what do you have to lose?

Newspaper journalists, like their radio and TV counterparts, are hungry for news – local newspapers and trade journals, particularly so. The first step, as with deciding where your customers are, is to decide what your audience reads, watches or listens to. A visit to your local library (or failing that, your nearest university library) should yield you access to one of the various media directories, which list every single publication, radio and TV station in existence, along with the names of their editors and producers.

Naturally, you won't be writing to all of them. Narrow the list down to publishers of journals or broadcasters of programmes whose audiences really would have an interest in your latest brilliant idea. Then (once you have done them the courtesy of finding out what their publication or broadcast is actually about) pick up the phone. Journalists very rarely bite – often, they are very pleased to hear from you.

If you are launching a new product or have reached some other milestone of interest to a wider public, the occasion may merit a press release. This is a document designed to do as much of the legwork as possible for busy journalists, by enabling them to establish very quickly the broad details of the story and whether it is relevant to their publication, as well as who to contact for further information (i.e. you).

Essentially, a press release answers the crucial questions: who, what, where, why, when and how. It should be clearly dated, double spaced and end with a contact name and telephone number. Ideally, it should not run to more than two pages. Vital information should be included in the first few paragraphs, supplementary detail should appear lower down.

You can send copies of your press release anywhere you think an editor or producer might be interested in it (for your own sake, you should avoid sending an announcement of your pioneering techniques in lace making to the *Pig Farmer's Weekly* – yes, it did exist, last time I looked, but you will certainly be 'spiked' and you will have wasted a stamp).

A good press release may be reproduced virtually verbatim in some publications; in others, a journalist will follow up the story and ask for more details. But don't leave them to do all the work. Following up yourself, with a phone-call, could help you make valuable contacts in the media, who may then come to regard you as a useful resource or spokesperson of their own. Sound familiar? Yes, it's networking again.

Another route is to follow up a similar story you've just read in the paper, by contacting the journalist whose by-line appears on the story. If, as often happens in national newspapers and magazines, that journalist specialises in a particular area, they'll be happy to know about possible sources of follow-up material or future features.

Keep the contact warm, but don't pester for coverage: this kind of relationship is an investment on both sides, and its time may come. So invest, and hope.

It does help if you can find an 'angle' that makes the story more intriguing, topical or timely. Think of some aspect of the work which is unusual; however excellent your product, there needs to be something a little different about it to attract attention in a world awash with me, me, me.

Particularly in trade journals, you may be offered the opportunity to take paid advertising to 'support' an editorial mention. Remember that if your story is good enough, there is no need to be pressured into accepting this offer. However, there is nothing wrong with doing so if you wish, although see below for tips on making your precious paid advertising work hard for you. And bear in mind also that somebody else raving about how marvellous your rubber grommets are, is worth any amount of self-advertising.

The media is one option. Another is to communicate direct with your prospective client, via the ubiquitous leaflet. People spend huge amounts of time on leaflets. (And even more time on logos. Logos are brilliant for avoidance.) It's great fun, but unless you are a professional graphic designer, that time is not invested wisely. Faced with the requirement to communicate above the babble of other voices in the marketplace, it's alarming how many people decide that fluorescent orange or green paper is the answer – producing a rather desperate effect.

Depending on what you want your leaflet for, you may be well-advised to invest in the services of that graphic designer – and possibly even a copywriter. If you're planning to mailshot hundreds or even thousands of potential clients, the very minimum that you want (in addition to a good mailing list) is clear, crisp, accurate communication. Direct mail is an expensive game, and you'll be competing for letter-box space with big players who have a lot of money to spend on elaborate design and colour photographs. Yours will have to stand out for other reasons.

On a smaller scale, in my opinion, there is no substitute for a simple business card and a great deal of legwork.

If you still want to produce a leaflet – to leave behind in libraries, on notice boards or, if you have the chance, to distribute as an insert in a trade magazine – don't talk about who you are. That's right. A client recently came bounding up full of excitement because he had been invited to place leaflets advertising his on-site massage service on the notice boards of a company employing some 8,000 people. What an opportunity! He showed me his leaflet. A long screed about who he was, where he studied, where he went to school. He would even have included the colour of his mother's eyes had there been room. I told him to tear it up and start again. 'What,' I asked him, 'are your potential customers going to be most interested in?' 'Well, they will be suffering from back strain from sitting at computers.' 'Good, so talk to their backs.' The leaflet was redone, this time asking people if they suffered from back or neck strain and saying, without embellishment, that relief was available. A phone number completed the simple message.

So, as a general rule, make all your promotional activity benefit-driven: the point is to focus attention on the potential customer and what you can do for them – not on you.

If you decide to advertise, choose very carefully where your few, highly expensive square inches will best bring results. Go through all the likely journals and see who else is advertising. What are they saying? What do you think of their advert? Is it a bit uninteresting or are you impressed? Try to be clear why. Providing they aren't your direct competitors, ring them and get chatting. You don't need to invent a story. Be honest, tell them who you are and that you are not a rival journal touting for advertising, say you were impressed by their entry and ask if it's been a success for them. Most people, once they know you are not selling anything, will be helpful and informative. You can save a lot of money this way.

As an advertising Portfolio Person, there will be the temptation to display all your wares at once. Don't. This is not a bazaar. Your message needs to be simple and direct. Don't diffuse its impact. As someone looking for an accountant, I may not be very interested in the fact that he or she also runs a rock band. In fact I might even be put off. You are going to have to place your various offers in different and appropriate shop windows.

If you have the budget, and want to reach a wider group of customers than your immediate locality, one way of advertising yourself very effectively is through a Home Page on the Internet.

It's also good to get into as many networking directories as you can – and learn how to use them. They are not lists for use as mass mail-outs, but a form of specialised Yellow Pages. And the point of Yellow Pages is that they are a resource. So, if someone asks you if you know anyone who's good at French translation, they obviously aren't a prospective customer this time round (unless that's you), but get your directories out and get recommending. That way, you please two people for the price of one. If everyone did this on a regular basis, they would have to do very little selling. If I was recommended as many times as I recommend, I would be unable to cope.

Networkers are natural communicators. That doesn't mean they have to be good at public speaking. But they do connect people with people. And rarely for gain. I know very few real networkers who want the traditional 10% cut of the deal. They're in it because they believe in it and because it works for them.

Which brings us back to self interest. Perhaps as we get older and wiser we can slowly transcend the illusion that the universe is there to revolve around us and begin to expect not just to get something from other people, but to give them something as well. It's a risky notion but interesting. Since we have more strings to our bows, we Portfolio People are better placed to try it out than most. It has to do with the Values Revolution I talked about before and whether it might be possible to put 'service' on an equal footing with 'profit'.

Profit?

Yes. Profit. We do have to make a profit in order to sustain our businesses, ourselves and our families. A profitable business is one which maintains itself well, has the means to invest in research and in better conditions for its people and one which can – if it chooses – invest some of its success in the community. Some people hate the notion of profit and it doesn't always get a good press these days. This is unrealistic. Money is the 'bottom line' for most of us, whether we like it or not.

Money is also the biggest cause of rows, matrimonial or business, and where we invest huge amounts of our anxiety. No wonder. Now that we have handed over so much responsibility to others for the supply of our needs, we are no longer, as individuals, able to fend for ourselves. Money has come to represent survival. Do you routinely fetch wood and lay a fire to keep warm, or bake your own bread? More likely, you pay for gas-fired central heating and buy your bread at the supermarket.

As our major preoccupier, money can thus be either the great enabler or the great underminer. It presses more buttons than the lift-operator at Harrods. You could read through this book agreeing with everything and put all the advice into practice and then, 'out of the blue', there arrives an innocent letter telling you your account is in the red at the bank. Your principles fly out of the window and in the

167

space of a few moments you experience shock, terror, anger and snarling aggression. As these feelings subside, you discover that you are left with all the resolve and *chutzpah* of a quivering jelly (lemon flavour).

In the next chapter, we'll look at ways of relating to money that serve you. You may not find them in the syllabus for a Practical Accountancy qualification but, as they're based on practical experience rather than theory, they will help you to deal with those debilitating feelings and, most importantly, to stay in control.

Chapter summary

- What do we want from other people – isn't there more to our relationship with them than that?
- Growing your own Fan Club – dispensing magic and light and investing your goodwill.
- The non-selective Fan Club – you can't afford to exclude *anyone*.
- How do you treat your Fan Club – how are you maintaining their loyalty?
- Knowing more about yourself and your personality and knowing more about others. Personality typing and how it can serve you.
- Body language – words only tell a small part of the story.
- When relationships go wrong – how to sort them out and utilise the difficulties as an opportunity for building an even better relationship.
- Being proactive with your relationships – don't wait for *them* to remember *you*.
- The absolute necessity of networking – being yourself and selling yourself, not what you produce.
- Promoting your products and services – the dreaded fluorescent flyer, successful advertising and getting your message across simply and effectively.
- Money as the great underminer . . .

Chapter Twelve

Financial footwork

We are moving from the specialist who is soon obsolete to the generalist who can adapt.

John Naisbitt, 'Megatrends' published 1982 by Warner Books Inc.

OUR TERMS OF PAYMENT VARY WITH ATTITUDE

– Sign on Accounts Office door, Sparks Automotive Ltd

WARNING!

As I said at the end of the last chapter, the advice that follows is not necessarily the kind that your accountant would give you, although I would like to think he or she would agree with most of it. You *should* see an accountant at least once, if only to help you set up your financial affairs in the way that serves you best, particularly from a tax point of view. Don't try to do it on your own.

WHERE ARE THE PROFITS IN YOUR PORTFOLIO?

In the last chapter we ended on the subject of profit. You have to make some profit, somewhere among your various businesses, even if some are in your portfolio for reasons other than financial gain. Let's go back to the 'Seven hour itch exercise' in Chapter 4 and do a similar one for your Portfolio Career. List the various activities in your Portfolio and score them on a scale of 1 to 10 for how fulfilling they feel, how much effort it feels as if you have to make for each of them. This time, however, be specific about how much actual time you put into them and how much money each activity makes, breaking it down so you can make 'like for like' comparisons. See the example below. Using columns 3 and 4, work out an hourly rate

WHAT'S WHAT IN YOUR PORTFOLIO?					
	1	2	3	4	5
Activity/Task/Job	Overall Fulfilment	Effort Involved	Time Required	Income £ S	Hourly Rate £ S

for each activity (4 ÷ 3 = hourly rate). Don't forget to allow for business expenses before calculating how much each activity 'nets'.

What does this exercise tell you? Are the most profitable activities in your portfolio also the most enjoyable? How much time are you spending on the most profitable activities? How much time do you want to spend on them? What could you improve? What could you jettison? Would you really miss it? Is it vital to your sanity or just a habit?

Try something called a 'sensitivity analysis', otherwise known as a 'What if?' exercise. What would happen to your profitability (*and* your peace of mind) if you did more of one thing and less of another? Or stopped doing something altogether?

Take time to do this exercise carefully – it can press hard on your anxiety and self-esteem buttons.

How did you get on? How many different scenarios did you try out? Were you really as bold as you could be? If you think you might have been a bit unadventurous, try one more but make it really loony, like giving up the steadiest item in your portfolio.

HOW MUCH TO CHARGE?

Deciding what to charge for your services presses lots of buttons too. Can you feel it now as you read this?

Among many of my clients, this is the area which causes more soul-searching, agonising and sheer terror than any other. So I have a simple formula for deciding what to charge, and a few basic rules.

The formula consists of an aggregate of three elements:

1. what the market will stand;
2. the perceived value of your service or product; and
3. your income needs.

What the market will stand depends on what people are used to paying. If there is a recognised rate for the job there is not much you can do to change it – but you should do all you can to find out what it is, what others are getting paid and what they are doing for the money. Or not doing. It's possible that your service is subtly different from theirs or that you are offering added value in some tangible way.

Perceived value is a fascinating subject. Many years ago I was talking to a market trader who had bought a huge box of cheap, plastic brooches. He had them on his stall for $2\frac{1}{2}$p (4 cents US) and no one was buying. He just couldn't shift them. Resisting the temptation to put the price down, he raised it instead. By 500%. He also removed the big box from sight and put out only a few brooches, on a velvet cloth. They started to sell.

I'm not for a moment comparing your skills and experience with cheap trinkets, but the point is, if you are asked by an multinational company to quote your day rate, they're not going to be too impressed if you come up with £50. They will be used to people charging £800 or more. If you go in too low they will see you as lightweight and low profile and you won't get the job. The rule when dealing with people handling huge sums of money, is to match their expectation and reassure them with an impressively high rate. Employing someone who is 'too cheap' is bad for their image, as well as raising questions (however unjustified) about the quality of

171

the work they are buying. Spending lots of money is a very important part of bolstering their sense of power, so help.

On the other hand, if you are pitching to a small, hard-up charity, they will be astonished by £150 a day and probably be put off by anything more than that.

It's important to know the culture you're pitching to, its image of itself, its habits and its attitudes around money. Are they tight-fisted – do they routinely query even reasonable expense claims? Do they expect to pay contractors a fair day's pay for a fair day's work – or do they screw them to the ground? Ask around, talk to people who know.

The third element, your needs, you should spend some time working out carefully. I would suggest the following way:

Calculate your personal financial needs over the year or a month, whichever is easier, remembering to include a level of income that delivers a good, nurturing lifestyle for you and your family. Planning for mere survival will only generate resentment and deplete your drive and enthusiasm, and that will show in your work. Who wants to employ someone who's always struggling?

Then work out how much gross income you need to generate per week to support all of this – including your operating costs (stationery, business phone, staff salaries etc) and your reserve or 'swimming' fund (explained below). By the way, the year for portfolio people shouldn't consist of much more than 45 weeks (roughly 6 weeks personal vacation and 1 week of public holidays. Yes, that much. Portfolio working uses up a lot of energy, which needs replenishing regularly). So if you need to generate, for example, a gross annual income of £33,750, that works out at £750 per week. Then divide this by three for your minimum day rate. In this example it comes to £250 per day. Why three? Remember the week in 3/2 time and all that scrubbing?

One further consideration: some weeks you may not get work for all your fee-earning days. One fashion photographer I know charges what at face value seems an extortionate amount per day – until you realise he may only be working four days a month. Also, a lot of 'invisible' time is spent on preparation, keeping equipment in trim, researching his shots and maintaining his knowledge of the fickle world of fashion.

So, now we've looked at the three elements, let's consider a possible scenario. There you are, sitting opposite the CEO of International Rubber Grommets Inc., faced with having to quote a day rate for consultancy. Your researches tell you that other experts in your field charge between £500 and £800 a day for this kind of work. Your conversation so far and, more particularly, your questioning, lead you to believe that the company is used to paying around £550 a day. Perceived value must obviously be more than that. Your needs are £450 per day. The likelihood of the commission turning into something long-term is quite high so you can cut your margins a bit. On the other hand that Rolls Royce Corniche in the car park is his – the receptionist told you when you asked admiringly – and you were recommended by a good mate of his. You do a one-second prayer, cross everything that's out of his sight and say, with utter conviction: £585 (not £600, that's too glib, £585 sounds thought about).

If you've impressed him, he'll probably say OK with a fair amount of nonchalance.

If he queries your figure, you can truthfully and convincingly say that this is at the lower end of the usual scale and that he could be paying much more, particularly if he went to one of those huge consulting practices with all their high overheads. If you have to give him a little 'victory', that's OK, but make sure it is little. Go down to £560, but stick there. Make sure he stays impressed.

Generally, there are three 'rules' around what to charge:

1. always quote more than you think, not less;
2. no freebies; and
3. no negotiating except *in extremis*.

If you go in high, you can always come down if you have to or if it's expedient, but do it for sound, tangible reasons, not out of charity. You don't want the customer to feel under-valued, or that they become 'second-class' clients by accepting. Talk about repeat business, guarantees of regular consultancy, long-term relationships and other 'good' reasons for reducing your rate. Remember their self-image and their dignity. And yours.

If you go in low, that's it. You'll never go up again. Your CEO who's used to paying more will doubt your abilities and find a reason to be unavailable for a year or two. Then there are those people out there who will love you for going in too low. They'll lap you up. Avoid them if you value your sanity. In my experience the people who expect to pay peanuts are the ones who give you the most grief, who ring late at night, who always change things at the last moment, who are the clients you need like a hole in the wallet.

Freebies are another danger zone. Avoid them unless you know the person asking for the favour really well, well enough to be certain that their intentions are good and that you can call on them later for a freebie yourself. The rule should be: if a prospective client wants you to do a free or – to use the common euphemism – 'speculative' piece of work for them, simply say you don't work in that way. That is an old ploy and one that could cost you a lot of money. A client of mine was called in to pitch for a number of design projects and found that he was invariably giving the prospect lots of great ideas and solutions to the company's problems – absolutely free. The prospects were happily milking him for ideas, taking copious notes and then saying 'we'll think about it and let you know.' They didn't. What they did was get someone in their organisation or an outside production artist to 'knock up' the work based on my client's ideas. He, naturally, heard nothing and then, some months later, saw his ideas all over the hoardings. He now charges a hefty fee for initial consultations, knowing that it is his creativity, imagination and knowledge of the client's market that, in that first highly focused meeting, can make or break a product launch.

So, if you are meeting such a potential client, tell them just enough about yourself and give them just enough imaginative responses to their problem to arouse their curiosity and get you the job. Remember to use the occasion to ask lots of questions; the client will expect you to and you'll stay in control of the meeting. If they want to talk solutions, there and then, inform them that you charge for ideas and solutions and you will have to invoice for the time. If the conversation 'sags' at this point and you get the feeling that you're losing it, ask more questions. Keep hold of the initiative, and if they show signs of wavering, bring in the 'deprivation principle'. This works on the basis that something which you can't have is infinitely more desirable than something you can have easily. So cut the conversation short, say you have another meeting. Release any expectation of closing the deal and tell yourself that they need you more than you need them (it may be true) – while continuing to 'think service' and what you could do for them. In this way, you project reassurance, stability, empathy and complete detachment – 'take it or leave it'. It often works, but expect to have to walk away from some of them.

174

The third rule, no negotiating, works on the same principle. People who are needy will be too prepared to negotiate and give in to demands for rates that will not serve them. You may be needy, desperate even, but remember, when you're tempted to say 'Yes, anything, anything!', that this is probably only a temporary state of neediness and when someone comes along who pays reasonably, you don't want to be lumbered with masses of your time committed to loss-making projects.

On the other hand, if there really is nothing else on the horizon, come down with as much grace and dignity as you can muster in the circumstances and treat it as an 'introductory rate', to apply only to the first phase of the work.

Knowing when to negotiate and when not is very much a matter for your intuition. So give it a chance to work, put off committing to a rate or fee until well into the meeting, until the prospect has shown as much as possible of their character. Don't be bamboozled, fazed or pressured. If in doubt, invent another project that you'll be hearing about in a few days' time and say you'll let them know when your diary commitments are clearer. Remember that pinch of cheek? When your back's against the wall is when to bring out your audacity. And charm. Never forget that.

Above all, don't allow your rates to be pushed down so low that your client ends up not respecting you. It's not a comfortable dynamic. One of the reasons, I believe, that the architectural profession has such problems getting its fees paid is that architects allowed themselves to be pushed too low in the first place. They lost respect. Compare the public's attitude to lawyers with their attitude to architects. In the UK very few people would countenance keeping their lawyer waiting for his or her fees: architects commonly wait six months. If you respect someone, you're more likely to pay them on time.

In the excitement of landing your contract, don't forget the essential paperwork: a letter from you to them confirming in every detail the terms of the deal and a purchase order or written confirmation of the deal – referring to your letter – from them to you. I shouldn't have to remind you that the more detail you note down now, while it's fresh in both your minds, the better, because if things go wrong later, you'll need all those little details carefully recorded when everyone else has forgotten them. Write your letter as soon after the clinching meeting as you can, preferably the same day. That way your confidence at having landed the 'job' will come through between the lines as authority and they'll respond appropriately.

There's one other consideration, and you'll probably only have one opportunity to clinch this – at that first meeting when the deal is agreed. That is . . .

MONEY UP FRONT

Lawyers do it. Stores do it. Why not you? When you get a particularly large commission, ask for a 'Mobilisation Payment' – a kind of deposit – and make sure that, in your terms and conditions or your confirming letter to the client, it states clearly that the payment is non-returnable if the project is cancelled for any reason or substantially re-briefed.

This may feel like an outrageous thing to ask. Why should it be? What you are really saying is that you are about to invest a large amount of your time in the project, to the possible exclusion of other clients and/or projects, and that you need a firm commitment from them too. Nothing is firmer than a big cheque.

Most reasonable clients will accept this principle, and quietly respect you for having the courage to ask for it. It is, after all, quite common. Lawyers rather cunningly refer to it as a fee for 'receiving instructions'. If your client won't pay you something 'up front', then you need to stage your invoicing carefully and prepare a payment plan (see below).

The next thing to negotiate is the size of the mobilisation payment. If the service you are providing is on a fixed sum basis, consider charging a percentage – I have sometimes managed 40% but 30% would be more realistic. If you are on a daily or hourly basis, try to agree a minimum number of hours as the basis for a mobilisation payment, based for example on how much time you've had to clear in your diary in the next few weeks to do the work or even just to prepare for it.

Think of the risks. To you, that is. How likely is the client to change his or her mind? What other factors are there that may cause a major change or cancellation? When might the axe fall? How much of your time are you likely to have expended on the project by the time it does? These are hypotheses I know, but err on the generous side – your side. Remember that business is always in a state of flux and that take-overs, mergers or a company launching itself on the stock market all make for a volatile state of affairs. I remember one very prestigious company commissioning me to carry out a specific piece of work. Somehow, despite all the boardroom meetings and enthusiastic handshakes from the CEO, it was always impossible to progress the project. There was always a very good reason why we should wait or review or re-think. Then the company went public and the project was axed. Although I have no doubt whatsoever that the client would have paid an invoice, I was glad of my mobilisation payment because I had done a lot of running around and had very little to show for it.

If you feel you won't ever be able to bring yourself to ask for this kind of payment, think of it in terms of a contract, a contract between your time and your client's money. Then see a cancellation in terms of a breach of that contract. Consider how your client would feel if, halfway through the project, you said you didn't have the time to complete it. Think how his lawyers would feel. Think, too, if your client cancels, of the extra time you'll need to spend finding something else – in a hurry – to fill that spare time capacity. What if, after making the time for the project and possibly turning other work down, the client cancels before it starts? Would they pay you something? It's unlikely – you haven't done anything tangible for them. Yet the project has already impacted on you and your time.

A mobilisation payment is also a powerful motivation to get on with the work.

PP Tip: When you're waiting in the potential client's reception and about to go in to clinch the deal, your mouth's dry, you're sweating rivulets and the coffee tastes awful, say the following mantra to yourself (under your breath, you don't want to alarm the receptionist): 'I'm the shopper, not the shelf.' Repeat it, often.

THE PAYMENT PLANNING POLKA

I cannot now remember the number of times I've turned up at clients' offices to find them gnashing their teeth and berating *their* customers. Why all the anguish? They forgot to arrange phased payments, they've done all the work, spent thousands on materials and staff salaries, haven't had a penny and now can't get paid until the client decides when he's going to complete the project and allow them to invoice. Or – and this is a old trick – the client finds a reason at the very last minute, when everything is done and dusted, to find fault with some quite trivial aspect of the work completed so far. It's a great way to deflect incoming invoices.

You may also have mused, whilst doing your cashflow in Chapter 6, how nice it would be if the income came in with the same unshakeable regularity as the bills. The very nature of Portfolio Working militates against this but there *is* something you can do about it, particularly with large or long-term contracts. It's called Payment Planning.

It will clearly help you if your fees are paid to you in regular instalments. It smoothes out the peaks and troughs of your income flow, you know where you are and what to expect and when and it means that you don't have to spend valuable time chasing *ad hoc* payments. It helps your client's accounts department as, once established, the payment becomes an accepted procedure. This is particularly true if the payment is made automatically by the client's bank. People in accounts departments love order, the knowledge that something is decided and that nothing more is required of them than to check that the figures are correct.

If you feel this would sharpen your negotiating skills, in your mind you could link the various payments from your portfolio of clients to some of the expenses you have. Amalgamated Consolidated's monthly instalment could be seen to cover the rent, International Rubber Grommets' weekly payment, the groceries. Linking the intangible with the tangible in this way is also an aid to your financial awareness, particularly when a contract is coming to an end soon and you need a cogent reminder to replace it.

Another aim of Payment Planning is to arrange, if you can, for your basic expenses to be covered by regular longer-term income and for 'one-off' or occasional consultancies to pay for non-regulars like holidays or computer up-grades.

Now we've looked at how to arrange your income to be as regular as your outgoings, let's look again at a cashflow projection.

KEEPING IN STEP WITH YOUR CASHFLOW

We looked at cashflows in Chapter 6. Look at yours again now and consider what you might change in the light of what you've read since then. Were you realistic enough with your expenditure predictions? Or your income? How does reviewing your cashflow influence the way you seek to be paid? Or how much you seek to be paid? Are there enough regular income payments to smooth your particular profile to manageable gradients? Or could you rearrange your payment on some items of expenditure, to more accurately mirror your income pattern? Things like regular quarterly payments – would making them monthly help tame your mountain range?

Spend some time playing with your cashflow. Sounds crazy, doesn't it? Never mind, try it. You'll be surprised.

One major consideration your cashflow should have highlighted is your tax bill. As a self-employed person, you'll be collecting your own tax and almost certainly handing it over to the tax man in six or twelve monthly lumps. If not planned for, this can be a severe test of your cashflow abilities and, for many people, of their relationship with their bank. If you can, put something aside every week or month for your tax, other major 'lumps' and contingencies. 20% of income would be a good proportion to start with. It may not be easy when money is scarce but start the habit, even if at the beginning it's only 20% of smaller items of income. Open a separate bank account, ideally one earning some interest, and start transferring – now. Call it your 'swimming fund', as opposed to the more usual 'sinking fund' – it's just a better image.

Use your cashflow. Cashflows come into their own with Portfolio Working. You're not reliant on one source of income and can juggle your income streams to ensure they flow evenly.

Review your cashflow regularly; 'regularly' does *not* mean once a year. Make it the basis of all your financial planning, of your major money decisions. Analyse your risks with it and then plan to avoid them. Design your spending using it, particularly if your accountant advises you, from a tax point of view, that you've got too much cash 'lying around'. Work on your cashflow with your accountant, using it as the basis for the agenda when you meet. Do not leave it on the shelf or in a pile. Have it with you at all times, even if your briefcase already feels full. It will serve you, if you'll let it.

THE SLOW PAYERS' SHUFFLE

There are always some people who take advantage of small businesses. They may be in financial difficulties but it's more likely to be their policy, part of their culture, to 'keep 'em waiting 'til they scream'.

If you've taken the time to build a good rapport – even a relationship – with the relevant person in Accounts, they are more likely to 'do you a favour', as they see it, if they like you than if they don't know you from Adam or Eve. Be courteous but firm. Eliminate the possibility that there is any other reason why your account is taking such a long time to settle. Establish very clearly that they are perfectly happy with your service and that it really is only an accounts matter. Check back with your records to see what their payment pattern is – you did record that, I hope – and, if they are 90 day payers, there's no point in chasing after three weeks.

If, after the payment pattern has been exceeded, whether it's 30, 60 or 90 days, you feel you've expended quite enough patience and it seems you are getting absolutely nowhere and being taken for granted, despite a number of friendly telephone or written reminders, offer to pick up a cheque personally, from the Chief Accountant. That sometimes works, if someone in the lower reaches of the Accounts Department has either lost or forgotten your invoice. If that doesn't work, tell Accounts you'll get onto the CEO. They don't like this. It disturbs their sense of order.

PP Tip: It's much easier – even quite exciting – chasing payments for someone else so try to get a personable and persistent friend to do it for you. They will have all the objectivity you lack, mixed with the determination, concern and righteous zeal of friendship. Besides, by now you may well come across on the phone as either pathetic or paranoid. Neither is conducive to extracting money from people.

If, after all this, still nothing happens, you can be sure that the company is either in a bad financial state or being run by people who, on reflection, you probably don't want to be doing business with anyway. So put the experts in. Professional debt-collection services can cost a lot less than you think, and it's worth paying a small percentage of the total outstanding to avoid turning yourself into a chainsaw-wielding maniac. It's well worth it for the peace of mind alone. Generally, people pay quite quickly if confronted by a large and insistent man leaning on their door frame and meaning-fully eyeing up their computer equipment for quick-sale potential. Remember, however, if you do decide to get 'heavy', you'll need evidence that they actually do owe you the money and this is where

180

your confirming letter from the first day, their confirming reply and a purchase order come in useful.

In the UK, one of the most effective ways of winkling out reluctant money owed to you is something called a Statutory Demand, effectively the first step in making a person or a company bankrupt. Here, you must be absolutely sure of your facts and be able to prove them. Also be prepared for the person or organisation to actually go under and for you not to get anything. For this reason, timing is critical. Before you go this route, find out what you can about their ability to pay, phone round some of their other suppliers if you know them and check out their experiences with the client.

Going to court for your money is expensive and hugely energy-draining. This is when you should seriously consider giving up and letting the whole sorry saga go. Even assuming you win the case – and this is by no means certain, however clear cut it may appear – nearly all your money could be gobbled up in legal fees. So this is very definitely a last resort. It's not really a solution, it's a game devised for lawyers. Avoid it if possible.

A last word of warning, based on someone's bitter experience. If you do arrange a payment plan with a client, stick to it. At the time, in the midst of the buzz of activity, it will seem easier and less unpleasant to carry on with the work even if your last invoices are very overdue for payment. The trouble is, once you've delivered the work, you've completely lost all leverage. So, awkward as it may feel, be very firm with your client and say that you are not able to deliver any further work or complete the project until the last invoices have been settled. I remember on occasion having to send architectural drawings cut in half to certain clients – they got one half and we kept the other – until they paid. Crude but very effective.

. . . AND THE CREDITORS' QUICKSTEP

As I said in Chapter 11 on Relationships, keeping in close touch with people you owe money to is also essential. Don't treat them the way some people treat you. It's all too easy to 'pretend' to yourself that they don't exist and ignore them. They should, in fact, be among your best business buddies because, as we've already seen, you will need to call on their extreme goodwill at some point. So don't treat them like wallflowers at the local hop. Dance with them. Let them know how things are for you, not just when it's tough but when it's going well. Share your triumphs with them – it's important that their image of you is one of achievement; you need their confidence in you. Because when you are in difficulties you will want them to see these in the larger context of your success. If they only experience you when you have problems, their image of you is not going to reassure them.

If you need to, put your cards on the table and explain your problem, be it a bad debt or a cashflow crisis. They will almost certainly have experienced these too and, if they know you well and like you, will probably be sympathetic and – most importantly – patient.

Don't wait until your creditors take steps from which it is difficult to retreat, even if they wanted to. Don't let things go too far. Too far is when other people with different agendas get involved and you lose control of the matter. I've seen people made bankrupt 'by mistake' because they failed to respond to the warnings their creditor had given, admittedly severe warnings but, nevertheless, only warnings. The creditor in one case was as shocked as the person he'd made bankrupt – and worried too, because he stood to lose a great deal of money.

Do have a firm proposal ready for when you meet your creditors. Remember that landlord? Part of something is better than lots of nothing. This and the 'I'll roll over and wave my legs in the air if you push me too hard' approach are effective with small and large creditors alike. The small business owners would generally much rather have something coming in every month than make you bankrupt. They are in the same position as you. The larger organisations, if approached with courtesy, honesty and timely initiative, will generally agree a deal too. But remember to show them some evidence that you can pay what you agree to and, if this is a cashflow 'blip' and things are clearly set to improve in a few months' time, say so. That way, they'll be more relaxed about giving you time. Worried people can turn aggressive and, in extreme circumstances, vindictive. Worried people tend to be the people who don't know what's happening. Having said that, don't make promises you can't keep. How will you know if you can? Yes, cashflow.

Remember, too, that the bank manager or tax inspector is likely to be more impressed by well-presented facts and figures than by vague promises and hopes. They will be pleased, flattered even, if they see that you've taken some trouble in preparing for your meeting with them. When talking to contractors on building sites and going through the drawings I'd prepared, I always found that if I'd made the effort to create good drawings (by which I mean clear, informative and accurate rather than merely 'pretty'), they responded to the effort and we had a much happier relationship and a better building as a result. So put some effort into it, even if things look dire. Be honest and realistic with yourself and, then, with them. This is where excellent records will not only come in handy in marshalling your facts and building your case – and being able to talk intelligently and authoritatively about it – but also in impressing the person you're asking for a stay of execution or a larger overdraft facility.

I never cease to be amazed how – after a little coaching – some of my clients then transform their relationship with a creditor in a single meeting, simply by overwhelming them with good, solid information. They go in expecting the end of the world and emerge having laid the foundations of a beautiful friendship.

Above all, don't wait for your creditors to call on you with the problem. Get there first so you can present it *your* way. Because they'll be expecting you to do quite the opposite, this will surprise and disarm them.

Surprise them too by treating them better than is the norm when things are going well. Don't just pay them on time. If you can – and this should be the aim of every business of any size – pay them as soon as you can. Yes, early. Why wait? Swap the miserly interest the bank pays you for the invaluable goodwill of your creditors – you may need it one day. I can already hear the account controllers and procurement experts collectively shuddering at the thought but I believe that a lot of businesses, especially small ones, would still be in existence today and providing an excellent service, if some of their clients had paid promptly rather than adopting a Scrooge-like attitude to what, in effect, was someone else's money. Don't be a bill-bully yourself and don't put up with it from others. If you pay your bills on time or early, you can reproach the slow payers with conviction.

If you find yourself having to negotiate with debtors trying to negotiate with you, try to build some sort of relationship with them, even if it is at the eleventh hour. Find out about them and their circumstances. This not only puts them more at ease (and therefore likely to divulge more of the true position) but it gives you better information on which to base your policy towards them. If they are being helpful and up-front about their situation, respect that. Remember how you felt in a similar position and how much courage it can sometimes take to tell the truth.

CHALKING THE DANCE FLOOR

All this talk of impressing people with wonderful and beautifully presented information is fine – providing you actually have it.

So I'm going to end this part of the book with some thoughts on record keeping that I've picked up or invented along the way. Some will be blindingly obvious and some frankly strange, but they work.

Remember that knowledge is power. If I had to say in one phrase what it was that brought some of my clients closest to ruin, it would be 'loss of control'. In the Never-Never Time I referred to in the Introduction to this book, whenever there was a problem, you just threw money at it. You employed lawyers, accountants and other experts and let them get on with it. While some people wore expensive jewellery, your average 80s businessman 'wore' expensive consultants as accessories. They hung around everywhere. It went with the culture.

This was all very well until the Reality came along and many businessmen were forced to fire the consultants and do it themselves. Some then discovered that they had absolutely no idea what was going on with their company. All manner of nasties suddenly crept out from behind the company woodwork: old unsettled debts, unresolved tax demands, obligations no one had warned them about, that had festered away and spread like dry rot in airless and unexamined corporate crevices. Of course, the high-powered advisors had long ago taken up fish farming in the Orkneys or gone native in Whakatane, well clear of any obligation to throw light (even if they could) on the confusion they'd helped to create.

I'd say it probably takes ten times longer to regain control than to create it in the first place. So be warned: employ an army of advisors if you will, but command them you must.

The way to command them (or to stay in control of yourself, if you're not using advisors all the time or at all) is to know the facts, primarily the financial facts, about your business at any one time.

Could you answer, without hesitation, these questions:

1. What is today's balance in your business account to within ±£50?

2. How much is your business owed right now?
3. How much does your business owe right now?

If you could, that's great. Many people can't. They have a low level of financial awareness.

As a Portfolio Person, you will need a particularly high level of financial awareness as all the normal complexities of being self-employed will be multiplied by the number of different activities in your portfolio. Your financial awareness needs to reach into all the corners, nooks and crannies of your businesses – regularly. Otherwise, that rot may slowly take hold.

You will therefore need to keep very good records, and know how to analyse them, how to spot in them any potential problems and how to use them to plan for the success of your business. You will need to be on top of your money or it will get on top of you.

Like most things, it's largely common sense. Nearly everything you need to do as a business person you can do yourself. Correction: you *should* be able to do yourself. The small number of very complex procedures, usually around tax planning, can be given to the experts but get them to explain. I have a rule, never to employ someone who can't explain the essentials of what they are doing for me. There are no exceptions, not even brain surgeons. Especially not brain surgeons. And there are some routine and time-consuming things, like book-keeping, that it's best to get help with.

The big problem is that most of us view keeping records with about as much enthusiasm as we have for filing.

The Golden Rule of Record Keeping: For Financial Health, Be Regular.

Below are one or two ways that are fairly painless and help you stay on top of your finances.

Running Cash Balance Book

Have you ever tried to work out in a hurry whether you have enough money in the bank for that new database package or another filing cabinet? Have you struggled for precious hours with cheque stubs and bank statements to find out? Help is at hand. Below is an example of what I call a Running Cash Balance Book ('running' in the sense that it's up to date, not 'running out'). A simple cash notebook will do, one that you can buy in most stationers.

You will see that it contains every credit and every debit from your business account and that every entry is then balanced. In this way, providing you keep it up to date on a daily basis, you know at any given moment exactly how much is in your account. You'll know before the bank. This is useful when you consider that statements can be as much as a month out of date. Regular 'automatic' payments in and out can be listed, with their relevant dates and amounts, at the beginning of the Running Cash Book so you don't overlook them in your calculations. Everyone I've introduced this system to turns out to be really surprised at how useful it is.

Bank reconciliations

These are a way of checking that your version of how much money

20·1·97	Brought forward	+	622	19	
21·1	Stationery	−	21	12	
		+	601	07	
21·1	Amalgated Consol. Inv. 356	+	950	00	
		+	1551	07	
22·1	Telephone Bill	−	237	82	
		+	1313	25	
22·1	Accountant Inv. A36/8	−	750	00	
		+	563	25	
24·1	Int. Rubber Grommets Inv. 341	+	2560	00	
		+	3123	25	
29·1	Transfer to Swimming Fund	−	700	00	
		+	2423	25	
31·1	Krazy Komputers Co	−	199	99	
		+	2223	26	
3·2	Bank payment – Rent	−	880	02	
		+	1343	24	

RUNNING CASH BALANCE BOOK

you have in the bank accords with their version, as set out in their statements. It is not *always* a foregone conclusion. There are healthy businesses based on locating banking errors. Reconciliations are, therefore, not only good for your peace of mind but also an essential part of accounting methodology. There are probably as many versions as there are accountants who, not unexpectedly, love them, so ask yours for a copy of his or her favourite and, too, for an explanation.

Your accounts

The core of your accounting records system consists of three items: your Analysis Book, your Sales Ledger and your Purchases (or Bought) Ledger. Even if you do nothing else, it is vital that you keep these three meticulously up to date, which means doing them regularly (or, better still, getting someone to do them for you – regularly. If you employ someone, make certain that you fully understand the system they adopt, whether manual or electronic and, if the latter, that you can operate the software just as well as they can.) One of the great benefits of the UK's Value Added Tax (VAT) is that everyone registered for it has to do their accounts at least every three months. I find it a wonderful discipline and I never thought I'd ever hear myself saying that. Three months is just about the limit of my recall on the details of my various financial transactions, so I don't miss much.

The Analysis Book is what it says: an analysis. It lists all your incomings and outgoings and in the latter case sorts them into different categories. That way you can see at a glance what you're spending on telephone bills, printing, fax rolls or taxis. This is essential information when, for example, you are doing a review and analysis of your spending patterns and how they are developing and changing over time. Below is a typical but simplified example of how an Analysis Book might be filled in. Remember that, whether they are just setting you up or staying as an ongoing member of your fan club, your accountant will have quite firm ideas about how to use an Analysis Book, so be guided by them.

Sales ledger

I prefer to call this my Invoices Out File but everyone is different. Whatever you decide to call it, it's a chronological list of all the invoices you produce and send to your clients. Together with the list (which I fill in every time I issue an invoice), I keep file copies of the actual invoices themselves in number order. Each invoice has its own unique consecutive number. If the file is kept up to date there will be no confusion over the number on the last invoice you sent out but, just in case, I also keep a list of numbers which I cross off one by one as I issue invoices with those numbers. This way I don't get in a muddle and send two invoices with the same number or jump numbers, neither of which are calculated to save time or your accountant's temper. The numbers of the invoices should be entered in the appropriate place in your Analysis Book.

I recommend putting as much information as possible on your invoices to clients. That way there is no excuse for a delay in payment, they have an opportunity to see clearly how you've calculated it and can compare it with your equally clearly produced fee proposal, almost certainly part of your confirming letter when the

JAN Date	CN°	To Whom	1/25	Office Supplies	Phones	Ca
6/f	—	—		117 01	27 22	119
1/1	261	Great Western Railways				
2	262	Acme Office Store		16 22		
4	263	John Smith	6/41			
8	264	Petty Cash				
8	265	Acme Office Store		24 63		
10	266	DIY Stores		37 17		
11	267	Wall to Wall Carpets		271 00		
13	268	Flashy Fotographic		29 99		
17	269	Premier Garages				89
17	270	Worldwide Mobiles			56 17	
17	271	Western Railways				
20	272	Premier Garages				11
21	273	Acme Office Stores		21 12		
22	274	Telecommunications Inc			237 82	
22	275	D Posit (Accountant)	A36/8			
29	—	Transfer to 0079264501				
31	276	Kvazy Komputers Co		199 99		
Total for January				600 12	299 99	20
Carried forward to February				717 13	321 21	323

ANALYSIS BOOK

188

project was first agreed between you. If you're smart, you can set up a pro forma on your PC which serves both as a fee proposal and an invoice. All you do is copy it, change the dates and headings, include any expenses and 'bingo'.

Purchases ledger

This I call my Invoices In file. Other people call it their Bought Ledger. Whatever you call it, the world being the way it is, this file is always much thicker than my Invoices Out file. Every invoice I get is kept in it, numbered as it is received with a unique, chronological number. This number also appears in the appropriate place in the Analysis Book.

Petty cash payments are recorded in a Petty Cash file and numbered too. As they don't appear in the Analysis Book, there is no confusion over numbering.

The point of all this is to make following money trails ('where it's gone', in layman-speak) easier and quicker. This helps everyone: your book-keeper, your accountant, your tax man but, principally, yourself. One of the most frustrating and time-wasting activities I know is trying to figure out confused accounts, and just because they're stored electronically doesn't make the situation any better.

A few other points to remember: keep every bit of paper to do with your finances: bills from shops, bus tickets, taxi receipts, train tickets, anything remotely financial. You'd be surprised how much you spend in cash and don't keep a record of 'because it's only a small amount and it's not worth it'. It really mounts up. Start a box into which you can tip everything. If it turns out to be a chocolate wrapper, it doesn't matter.

If you do your accounts electronically, keep hard copies of everything and back up onto disk daily. Keep your disk away from your office if you can and, if it's particularly sensitive or valuable data, keep it with you at all times in your briefcase. This applies to all important documents. Imagine if your system crashed and you couldn't prove a vital agreement with a difficult client or supplier. When you've let your imagination rip and thoroughly scared yourself, start hard copies and back-ups for everything. For the seriously careful, think about investing in a fire-safe, and/or external archiving.

It hardly needs saying that the quality of your financial record keeping will directly impact on your sanity and, because time costs money, your bank balance. Despite the crassly obvious truth of this statement, many people keep appallingly bad records and pay huge amounts to their accountants once a year to have them sift through plastic bags full of jumbled up receipts and other bits of screwed up paper. So love your accountant – don't turn them into a bag-person.

THE LAST WALTZ

There is a lot of fear around money. Many of the problems we've touched on in this chapter would hardly exist were it not for fear. Fear of not succeeding, fear of not being good enough, fear of not being paid, fear that we won't have enough money, that we'll lose what we have and, if we *do* have lots of it, fear that someone will try to steal it from us.

Money has become the umbilical cord which connects us to well-being. Without it we can't eat, have shelter or clothe ourselves. Sometimes you even have to pay to pee. We have exchanged our ability to provide for ourselves with the ability to pay others to do it for us.

More importantly, in the 'developed world' where most people can confidently tick off large chunks of Maslow's hierarchy of need, our preoccupation is not with survival but with image. It's no longer enough just to eat, however well. We have to be seen to be eating the right food, out of the right packaging or in the right restaurant, with the right people. Industries invest not just in producing goods but in convincing us that we need them. Fair enough, you might think, but the reality of this is that they thereby dictate where we live, where and when we shop, what we drive, wear, smoke, drink or watch. As Francis Kinsman points out, only a few of us, the 'inner directeds', are reasonably immune to these pressures to conform to a 'manufac-tured' normality.

If we followed the recent example of somewhere like, for example, Albania where, if you wanted a freezer, there was one model available and that was it, all this pressure would be bad enough, but it is compounded by the huge number of competing and conflicting messages. We are victims of the tyranny of choice, and of those who seek to guide us to the 'right' decisions.

Consequently we are fearful of looking wrong, of not being hip or streetwise, of being out of touch, old, slow, boring, uninformed. It's no longer a case of being on one treadmill, many of us are trying to straddle half a dozen. We are devouring an ever-increasing, ever more complex diet of new experiences. All this munching, digesting and defecating of novelty requires one basic resource: money. Enough money will ensure that (for the moment) we have the most desirable residence, the shiniest car, the smartest clothes, the latest techno-toys, that we see the trendiest movie premières and sit in the best seats at the opera. Excessive and very overt spending is a way of avoiding choice.

The reality may have slowed the mills a little but the rush to catch our own tails is still on. Is it any wonder we have so much fear around money?

One of my personal aims now is to replace as much as possible of my dependence on others – through money – with dependence on myself for the important, material things in my life. While there is much that I cannot change, there are also things in which I can become self-sufficient. They start with my thoughts, my curiosity and my personal perception of the balance between my material and spiritual wants and needs. The list continues with how much I am prepared to collude with 'accepted' convention – I have no television, I don't eat hamburgers and I only wear a suit at weddings, christenings and funerals. (And I walk to the shops.) In the future I would like to be able to supply my own energy, my own entertainment (solo violin performances only – absolutely no scrubbing), grow my own food, be increasingly responsible for my own health and even build my own house.

Freeing myself from the umbilical cord that someone I've never met wants to attach to me leaves me feeling, not isolated or exposed, but actually safer, more in control, less fearful. The fear that is being fed through that cord, along with the 'goodies', begins to diminish. (In case you think I've joined the Luddites, I *will* be on the Internet.)

What might happen if the whole World of Work began to do the same? More importantly, what might happen to Portfolio People – and specifically, you? We'll look at this now, in the last part of this book.

Chapter summary

- Locating the profits in your portfolio – what makes most money, what gives most fulfilment, what you could drop or scale down.
- How much to charge – the basic formula: what the market will stand, perceived value and your income needs.

- Quoting up rather than down, making yourself a freebie-free zone and avoiding negotiation if you can.
- Essential paperwork once you've landed the contract – confirming letters and purchase orders.
- Getting paid up-front – having the nerve to ask the unthinkable and why it's fair dinkum.
- Planning your payments so you don't leave getting paid to the very end – when you are most vulnerable – and so your cashflow landscape looks like Holland, not the Rockies.
- Using your cashflow as a basic planning tool for your business and creating a 'swimming' fund for contingencies.
- How to deal with slow payers – combining patience with knowing your rights, legal realities and being a good payer yourself.
- Putting the boot in when you have to.
- What to do when you are in financial difficulties and can't pay your creditors – being proactive and presenting the facts well, however awful.
- Complete knowledge of your businesses' finances is power and control – have it and you are virtually unassailable, lose it and you're terribly exposed.
- Running Cash Balance – knowing how much you've got in the bank, minute by minute, before they do.
- Bank reconciliations – they don't always get it right.
- Your accounts – Analysis Book, Sales ledger and Purchases ledger: the three vital components of any business's financial control.
- Keeping everything, every scrap of paper to do with money, but taking pity on your accountant – and yourself – by sorting it out regularly.
- The fear that hangs around money like a fetid fog – the umbilical cord of need that we're all attached to, the importance of image, the tyranny of choice and the way back to self-sufficiency and serenity.

PART FOUR
WHERE AND WHAT NEXT?

An opportunity to draw breath long enough to consider what happens next in your life . . .

To attain knowledge, add things every day. To attain wisdom, remove things every day.

Lao-tzu

Chapter Thirteen

The next ten years

Go confidently in the direction of your dreams! Live the life you've imagined. As you simplify your life, the laws of the universe will be simpler; solitude will not be solitude, poverty will not be poverty, nor weakness weakness.

Henry David Thoreau

You've read the book. You may already be in a Portfolio Career. What happens now?

We do a final check. In your pad write down all the things you want to have happen in your life – use your visions list in Chapter 4 as a base if you like.

Now write a list of the things you need to do to in order for them to happen. It may be that having a Portfolio Career is not the right place to start. It may be ideal. Be terribly honest with yourself.

If you decide that your Portfolio Career is the right vehicle for your growth or that you will embark on one very soon, here are some of the essentials for maintaining it:

- Be curious about everything around you, how it works but also *why* it works. Become a questioner, be interested, be prepared to appear ignorant, give others the opportunity to display their knowledge and skill.
- Trust that there is a need for your creative talents and skills. We are all immensely gifted with knowledge, ability and – if we listen to it – wisdom.
- Focus on doing the task beautifully, however simple or unglamorous, not on the money you'll be paid for it. That will follow.
- Network yourself, give space to others networking and always look for opportunities to help others through your contacts, ideas and encouragement. Remember the theory of karma but don't expect instant results.

- Motivate yourself through constant evaluation of why you are doing what you are doing and how it is serving you, even in the very simplest and most humble way.
- Review yourself regularly, lovingly and honestly. Acknowledge the child in you that needs your love, your support, your guidance. Then provide it without question.
- Manage your time. Value it as a precious resource to be given as a gift to others – and yourself. Give this gift to yourself as often as you can: arrange to have regular 'me-time' days, like birthdays, but far more frequently.
- Know what is happening in your Portfolio of businesses, particularly in relation to money. Examine your money, acknowledge it and honour it for the resource it is and try not to fear it. Get it in perspective with the rest of your life.
- Use your knowledge of your businesses to plan for success, to plan for balancing change and novelty with stability and contentment. Grow work for yourself and have the positive experience of work grow you.
- Be alone regularly and in a quiet space.
- Make space for the cleansing action of passive thoughts; listen to your intuition.
- Expect and welcome transformation, in you and in the world.
- Revisit your visions.
- Enjoy.

If this seems like an awful lot to be doing as well as the actual work, it is. But, with practice, it will become second nature, like driving or brushing your teeth. Or making back-ups. Think back to your first day at school or your first driving lesson. It probably felt as though you would never get to know all those rules, all those pedals, knobs and levers. Now? No problem.

So don't rush it. Savour each step. Portfolio Careers are to be enjoyed.

Finally, if ever you feel you are not getting the most out of your Portfolio Career, go back a step. Examine what you did before this step, how well you prepared for where you are now. Is there something you rushed or overlooked or – dare I say it – avoided? Something you don't like doing very much – like financial planning? Or diary management? When did you last stay in bed all morning? All day? How is your fan club? When did they last hear from you? When did you last really *do* lunch as opposed to talking about it?

Use the bullet points at the end of each chapter as a check list in order to re-examine your strategies and decisions.

And if you don't want to be a Portfolio Person any longer? Fine.

Everything has a cycle and there is no shame in stopping being a Portfolio Person. Use your portfolio career as a springboard from which to reach other opportunities. Take the richness of the experiences and bring them to bear on finding a full-time position. Take your light along to interviews and shine. Project your stability and your flexibility. Be curious and cheeky. Remember who's the shopper, who the shelf.

Bring your Portfolio skills as a precious gift to your new job when you've secured it. You will almost certainly find it more satisfying after a Portfolio Career because you will be bringing more than a methodology to it, you'll be bringing an attitude. Treat your full-time job as a Portfolio Career in itself. Apply the 'rules' set out in this book. Be the 'can do' person in an often 'can't do' environment. But remember that not everyone will understand the Portfolio outlook, so tread lightly.

Gillian Edwards, one-time Portfolio Girl of stage, page and screen, now has one single income-generating activity and she loves it. She is applying her Portfolio attitude to her full time job and experiences it as being richer and more fulfilling as a result. Through her curiosity and 'can-do' attitude, she is finding more in her job than before, more that needs doing, more to enjoy. Her colleagues experience working with her as rich and fulfilling too.

There are so many opportunities now to apply the Portfolio attitude, whatever type of work you do. It is equally applicable to retirement or to the very beginning of a working life, to those currently without work and to those with one or more part-time activities. Downshifting, voluntary simplicity, opting out of the 'rat-race', 'feeling the quality not the width', putting the 'ful' in front of 'filling' – all are now top of the work agenda. Writers like Handy, Kinsman, Fox and others are read and respected in staid business journals and alternative magazines alike. The readers may love what they say, they may not. But they do read them. There is a hunger for meaning in what we do, for something other than chasing our tails.

I believe Portfolio People have a better chance than most to step off a few of the treadmills I spoke of in the last chapter and begin the process Charles Handy calls 'rediscovering the soul', the process by which our need to create and to contribute can be recognised and fulfilled, and our deep longings can be satisfied. As His Holiness the

Dalai Lama said, 'a person who is not content is poor'. Both he and Handy agree that the time has come when each of us will have to define our personal 'enough', the point at which we'll stop playing the Fisherman's Wife and embrace inner as well as outer growth.

Portfolio People have the breadth of vision, the grasp of the coming reality, that taste of something new and exciting on the tongue that will give them the courage and audacity to play a major part in the dismantling of our carefully marketed, pre-packaged, rationalised and bar-coded mediocrity. As they network themselves, they are already networking a different vision, a more caring and satisfying way of being, a workstyle that is not only about work. It may well be the beginning of a kind of Wholonomy. We will see.

Remember that question right at the beginning of this book? You may have missed it – not everyone reads Prefaces – so here it is again: Why do you work? Answer it now.

I hope that this book has given you something to think and feel about, some tangible help and, most of all, clarity about what it is like to be one of the blossoming band of Portfolio People.

Grow well!

BIBLIOGRAPHY

We can't afford to leave our spiritual and ethical values in the company parking lot when we come to work ... because nation states are no longer in control – business is.

Richard Barrett, World Bank Spiritual Unfoldment Society

This is a list of books I've read or – if I'm honest – in some cases partly read and which have interested, influenced, excited or moved me. They all have something important to say about the human condition, whether expressed in stories, life experiences or rational concepts. It's not a long list, partly because I find long bibliographies a bit intimidating and partly because my reading for this book was quite modest and the material in it is largely my own.

I have also attempted a paragraph on each book as a very inadequate and unashamedly personal 'taster' but one which I hope will whet your appetite for more.

'Jobshift' by William Bridges, published 1990 by Nicholas Brealey Publishing
A very thorough and readable explanation of the background to the Job as we have understood it traditionally, its current demise and what will replace it. Bridges gives a lively and – despite the massive changes he points up – above all encouraging picture of what most of us will be doing if we want to be part of the 21st Century. Excellent advice, patient explanation and (thank goodness in a 'business' book) some humour.

'Megatrends' by John Naisbitt, published 1982 by Warner Books Inc
Alarming and compelling, an exposition on ten colossal trends afoot in the world, including the metamorphosis from industrial to information society, national economy to world economy, short term

to long term, institutional to self help and hierarchies to networking. Don't read this before you go to bed, you won't sleep.

'The Age of Unreason' by Charles Handy, published 1990 by Arrow Books Limited

Handy takes our common perceptions by the scruff of the neck, shakes them without mercy and explains to us what falls out and why. A master at finding and – above all – explaining paradox in our lives, to the point where we cannot imagine why we didn't see it ourselves. He is surely possessed of a magic looking glass, from behind which he conjures disturbingly plausible inversions of contemporary ways of thinking. Despite being promoted as a business book, it is nothing of the sort, but a book about our values, our life's purpose and how we might rediscover them both again.

'The Empty Raincoat' by Charles Handy, published 1994 by Hutchinson

Having astonished and alarmed us in *The Age of Unreason*, Handy finds yet more explanations for the way our society is moving and gives them absurd but deadly accurate names – the Sigmoid Curve, the Doughnut Principle and the Chinese Contract are a few notables. He seeks to design an alternative universe, one based on a sense of purpose, of direction and groundedness. Inspiring and relieving, since he gets to our most compelling concerns, converts them brilliantly into extraordinary paradoxes and then proceeds to point to viable – if unusual – ways to realise solutions to them.

'Millennium' by Francis Kinsman, published 1990 by W. H. Allen & Co.

At a time when most of us were on Greed Mountain, clambering over each other to reach the promised Never-Never Land before it disappeared, Kinsman was not only pointing to the consequences of our collective folly and the harsh choices we had created for ourselves, but also to the beginnings of what could be the dawn of a brighter, saner age. He talks of those people who are not affected by the image creators and style merchants, the 'inner directeds' whose personal values come from within themselves, not from a glossy magazine or prime time television. This is an uncompromising, yet gentle and encouraging book and, to my delight, concludes with one of my favourite fairy tales, the story of Stone Soup.

'The Reinvention of Work' by Matthew Fox, published 1994 by HarperSanFrancisco

Fox turns the notion of why we work on its head. Challenging the idea that unemployment is acceptable and pointing to the commonly experienced feelings of isolation, insecurity, alienation and, above all, purposelessness in our work lives, he proposes a world where inner work – that 'world within our souls' – and outer work are in balance, where work allows a simultaneous experience and development of both. This book will confront your assumptions around the purpose of working, the 'quick-fix' call for jobs, jobs and more jobs and disturb your notion of what we are here to do.

'Small is Beautiful' by E. F. Schumacher, published 1973 by Vintage

This book has to be one of the few truly groundbreaking works of this century. Schumacher exposed and questioned comfortable conventions at a time when few others had any idea – or particularly cared – where society was heading. He challenged the doctrine of economic, technological and scientific specialisation, proposed smaller working units, communal ownership, regional workplaces and encouraged ubiety, a strong sense of locality, of relationship with and investment in a place. Despite being over twenty years old, this book is still spot on.

'Towards Social Renewal' by Rudolf Steiner, published in 1992 by Rudolf Steiner Press

An infuriatingly difficult book to read; one looks to the translation to lighten the rather heavy, early 20th Century German prose but it fails and the concepts seem therefore doubly difficult to grasp. Nevertheless, it is an extraordinary work and one that repays persistence since it is achieved through deep spiritual insight and is thus truly original and free of anything remotely recognisable as conventional rationale. Remarkable – and yet not surprising – to think this was being written in the context of a thoroughly rigid social order born of Victorian values and injured German national pride.

'Creating Abundance' by Andrew Ferguson, published in 1992 by Judy Piatkus (Publications) Limited

Andrew Ferguson talks of that 'temporary aberration', the Industrial Age, calls for an end to unchecked growth and argues that money and affluence are not the primary measures of success in life. Having worked with Andrew at the Breakthrough Centre in London, I am particularly grateful for his excellent and clear development of the 'seven levels', a devastatingly simple and yet effective model for grounding vision into successful action and, too, for his almost single-handed quest for the actual – as opposed to theoretical – combining of spirit and business. Andrew was doing it when most people were just thinking about talking about it.

'The Gaia Atlas of Planet Management', published in 1985 by Pan Books

Irrefutable evidence, if any were needed, that rather than merely evolving as a planet, we are now on a collision course with our destiny. We have really reached the point where life at this pace and this scale is no longer sustainable. Simple mathematics shows this to be true. This book chooses to make the point with lively yet carefully researched illustrations. Essential Christmas present material for any child. Essential reading for anyone who ever wonders how it will be when there are more roads than there are fields. This is not such a daft notion. Read Handy, Naisbitt and a host of others if you don't believe me.

'Ritual. Power, Healing and Community' by Malidoma Patrice Somé, published in 1993 by Swan Raven & Company

An extraordinary book which spans two utterly different worlds and explains the increasingly vital connection between them. Somé was initiated in the ancestral tribal traditions of Burkina Faso, is a medicine man and diviner in the Dagara culture, holds three master's degrees and has two PhDs. He shows, through his own and others' stories, the importance of ritual in our lives and how the western Machine Age has blinded us with a more comfortable, more convenient lifestyle while at the same time robbing us of meaning and self-hood. This book touches deep into longings we may not have known we had.

'The Alchemist' by Paulo Coelho, published in 1995 by Thorsons

A magical story of the Possible. Proof of the importance of stories as a means of passing on knowledge, understanding and wisdom. The inspiration to believe in yourself and your destiny, and then act on it. Essential reading (and re-reading) for Portfolio People.

'The Green Fairy Book' Edited by Andrew Lang, published in 1965 by Dover Publications Inc.

Legends, myths and fairy tales are the world's great Library of Wisdom, these days rather under utilised in the face of Mutant Ninja Turtles and other 'instant' gratifications with all the lasting benefits of a burger. By eschewing simplicity as too dull or repetitive, we deny ourselves an understanding of what we are here to be. So, turn off the telly and tune in to truth with a fairy tale or two.

'The New Leaders' magazine, published bi-monthly by Sterling & Stone Inc., San Francisco

A regular diet of reality and inspiration. Very much on the ground, this publication offers some of the latest thinking and experience from the US on balanced business.

'Resurgence' magazine, published bi-monthly and edited by Satish Kumar

Many so-called 'alternative' journals shoot onto the scene in a shower of sparks and then fizzle out. Resurgence has simply glowed, steadily and reliably, since it began in 1966, shining its kindly but penetrating light on all aspects of life. It is normal, almost expected now, to find an article by Charles Handy on the doctrine of 'enough' alongside one on the Buddhist teaching of 'Right Livelihood'. Beautifully produced, it never fails to deliver new insights, old wisdom and hope. Thanks, Satish.

Index